Banishing Bullying Behavior:
A Call to Action

From Early Childhood Through Senior Adulthood

Banishing Bullying Behavior:
A Call to Action

From Early Childhood Through Senior Adulthood

Blanche E. Sosland, Ph.D.

DEDICATION

To the blessed memory of my parents, Kate Simon Eisemann and Moses Max Eisemann, Ph.D., refugees of Hitler, who built new lives in the United States. In gratitude for the legacy of love, learning, discipline and decency they left for the generations that have followed them.

PRAISE FOR
"BANISHING BULLYING BEHAVIOR"
AND FOR DR. BLANCHE SOSLAND

Bullying means different things to different people and overlaps with a lot of other terms, such as domineering, intimidating, persecuting, oppressing, tormenting, harassing, assaulting, forcing, and compelling. It involves a power imbalance, wherein the bully can force a person to behave in a way he or she does not want to because of the superior size, strength or position of the bully.

We have traditionally thought of bullying as "unwanted aggression," directed toward children or teens by other children or teens, but it has become increasingly clear that it is pervasive in our society. It happens in our families, in our schools, in our workplaces, in our local, state and federal governments, and even in our churches. It happens to children, teens, adults, and senior citizens, and among all ethnic groups and genders. It is serious and, at best, divisive. It can completely disrupt the lives of individuals and families, and, at worst, lead to suicides among children, teens, and adults.

Dr. Blanche Sosland has been involved in the workplace as a long-term employee of Park University. In addition to her family's extensive business interests, she has had consulting and numerous other contacts with business and governmental leaders. In fact, business leaders asked her to write a book on bullying in the workplace after reading some of her works on bullying in schools. Her long-time involvement in numerous community organizations also adds to her broad-based perspective.

Much of the literature to date has been on bullying among children and teens, but it is past time that we look at the big picture, the common elements, and what can be done to cope with it, and better yet, to prevent it. I am pleased to endorse this book because it takes such a comprehensive approach.

I am also pleased to endorse Dr. Blanche Sosland. I had the privilege of working with her for fourteen years and have known her for thirty years. We often strategized together to, over time, build the very large and high-quality Education Department at Park University. Blanche was a highly esteemed Professor at Park University, esteemed by me as the current

President, by her supervising provost, by her faculty colleagues, and by her students. She was also respected by her colleagues in the metro and across the state as a leader in the education community.

Students loved Blanche for her interest in them as individuals, but also for her interesting lectures, especially appreciating her "real life" illustrations. They knew that her course content was contemporary, even "cutting edge," yet would be based in sound theory and best practice. They enrolled in large numbers, knowing that course content would be relevant, even though they also knew that course requirements would be demanding.

These attributes are among the reasons I believe Dr. Blanche Sosland is the ideal person to write this much-needed comprehensive approach to bullying. She has read the literature and taught classes on bullying for many years, and has consulted, lectured, and published on the topic. Her wisdom, her ability to synthesize what others have written, her ability to analyze contemporary problems, to see solutions and articulate them are remarkable.

I am certain this book will be a valuable resource for all who are concerned about either learning about bullying or, better yet, doing something about it.

Donald J. Breckon, Ph.D.
President Emeritus, Park University

CONTENTS

Foreword	Marc Solomon	vi
Introduction	Jane Clementi	ix
Preface		xii

Chapter One — A Call to Action 1
Discussion of Sioux City Editorial Board call to action, what it represents and the need for response.

Chapter Two — Bullying Continuum from Early Childhood through Senior Adulthood 9
Discussion of bullying behaviors at all stages and putting them into context.

Chapter Three — What Prompts a Former Bully to Tell His Story? 23
One bully shares his decades of bullying behavior into adulthood to help people understand the pain of a bully and the importance of early intervention.

Chapter Four — Overview of Workplace Bullying 35
Presentation of the scope and depth of workplace bullying.

Chapter Five — Bullying in Specific Workplace Venues 49
Discussion of how bullying in specific workplaces plays out and what can be learned from the shared experiences.

Chapter Six — Leadership, Leadership, Leadership 58
Discussion of healthy workplace settings.

Chapter Seven	**Cyber Bullying: Peer Abuse in its Most Lethal Form** 65	
	An in-depth discussion of cyber bullying at all stages of peer abuse.	
Chapter Eight	**Senior Adult Bullying** 77	
	As our population ages, the "once a bully, always a bully" emerges as a serious concern.	
Chapter Nine	**The Enormous Power of Kindness** 90	
	The role of modeling and teaching kindness as an important component of the solution to the bullying problem.	
Chapter Ten	**Model Responses to Call for Action** 99	
	Description of several organizations' response to the call for action and guidelines for individual and group responses.	
Appendix	 110	
Acknowledgements	 126	

FOREWORD

Growing up a gay kid in Kansas City in the 1970s, I was the victim of bullying in both direct and indirect ways. Directly, I remember going to big social gatherings of my Jewish youth group in high school and being petrified that a small group of boys would seek me out and make fun of me for being gay. Every time I'd enter the room, I would look around with vigilance for these boys, hoping they wouldn't be there that night or at least wouldn't notice me. Indirectly, I made decisions to conform, to be the boy I was "supposed to be," rather than following my own instincts, out of fear of being teased for being different. Dolls and knitting went by the wayside, and football and basketball became priorities. I can see now that every time I turned away from following my instincts, I was accepting the notion of the bully — that there was something wrong with who I was.

I also recall being a bully myself, joining others in taunting a girl who was going through a tough time in junior high school. And I recall observing bullying and doing nothing about it. My freshman year of high school, I vividly recall boys picking on a very effeminate kid in geometry class and the teacher joining in and laughing at the kid.

It took me a long time to gain the confidence to come out of the closet, finally doing so at the age of thirty. By then, I was working as a political organizer and strategist, and I eventually turned my focus full-time to the fight for marriage equality for same-sex couples.

Among my motivations for dedicating myself to that fight, which I stuck with for more than a decade, was the notion that I didn't want kids to have the same difficulties that I had in coming out and accepting who they are. I believed strongly that if same-sex couples could marry, then no matter how much gay kids might be bullied in their schools, stigmatized in their faith communities, or demeaned in their homes, they would know that their government was on their side when it came to respecting the validity of their love. It would be a powerful antidote.

In *Banishing Bullying Behavior: A Call to Action,* Blanche Sosland has written a powerful book that will make a real difference in the lives of LGBTQ people and so many others who are stigmatized or viewed by society as "less than" for one or myriad reasons.

I've known Blanche for nearly my entire life. Her son was one of my best friends growing up (and still is), her daughter taught my health class in elementary school, and her son-in-law led my summer high school pilgrimage to Israel. Blanche's family is one of the most generous I know, focused relentlessly on bringing kindness and healing to our world. And so, it is no surprise to me that Blanche has taken her expertise from the academy — where she served as a Professor of Teacher Education at Park University for many years — and her years of civic pursuits in Kansas City and focused them on combatting bullying.

Banishing Bullying Behavior speaks of the pervasiveness of bullying. It can be physical or verbal. It can happen face to face or through cyberspace. It can happen in every cycle of our lives in settings where people are vulnerable: school, home, the workplace, and senior living. And it's a behavior that is in many cases passed from generation to generation.

What I love about this book is that it is — as its title suggests — very much a call to action. "The cycle of this behavior," Blanche writes, "is one that needs to be broken." Blanche describes different systemic interventions that are helpful in stopping bullying. But, she explains, it's not enough to leave it to impersonal systems and institutions to combat bullying. She highlights the imperative for every one of us to leave our comfort zone, step up, speak out, and take action. Ultimately, she argues, ending bullying is not a spectator sport. It's a moral pursuit, where individuals tap into internal sources of kindness, love, and courage and work to create an environment where bullying isn't tolerated and where each of us is doing our part.

Blanche's challenge is one I take to heart. Now that the marriage equality fight is over, I'm working to take lessons from that effort to pass laws to combat oppression and bullying against other marginalized groups, including immigrants, whom President Donald Trump — whom Blanche accurately calls our "Bully-in-Chief" — attacks and bullies with ruthless cruelty.

If all of us follow Blanche's prescription, we can bring about my deepest aspiration for the LGBTQ community. My hope is that the notion of coming out — which I struggled with for many years — disappears. Kids — as they recognize they are or might be gay, lesbian, bisexual, or transgender —

would simply talk about their sexual or gender identity in real time because there is no stigma. It would be as simple as "coming out" as left-handed.

Blanche challenges everyone to be courageous with their kindness, and she explains that in doing so, we can bring about a world where stigma of every sort dissipates and evaporates and kindness and love prevail. "The power of kindness," she writes, "can't be underestimated in our work to prevent bullying behavior and in our response to it."

Let's get to work and make it so!

Marc Soloman
Author
Winning Marriage: The Inside Story of How Same-Sex Couples Took on the Politician and Pundits — and Won (2015)

INTRODUCTION

It is an honor to be included in Blanche Sosland's book *Banishing Bullying Behavior: A Call to Action From Early Childhood Through Senior Adulthood*. I welcome adding my voice to the many that recognize this serious epidemic of poor, mean-spirited, and aggressive behavior that is so pervasive in our society today. We can never have too many conversations or voices speaking up and calling out these negative bullying behaviors, as we might never know whose voice will speak to whom or what will spark a change in someone.

My hope is that this book will create a change in many more than just one, as this topic of bullying is so very personal and near and dear to my heart. In September of 2010, my son Tyler Clementi made national headlines, not for his musical gifts or his thoughtful kindness, but rather because of a decision he made after he had been targeted by his roommate in the cyber world. A decision that was made at a very dark, lonely, and desperate time, which twisted Tyler's reality and blinded him to the resources and support that he had available to him both at school and at home. It was a permanent decision to a temporary situation. On September 22, 2010, Tyler died by suicide. He was only eighteen years old.

As much as my husband, Joe, and I would like to go back and change Tyler's actions and decision, the reality is we cannot. That is why we created the Tyler Clementi Foundation to put an end to all online and offline bullying and to add our voices to the conversations started by Tyler's headlines as well as all the other headlines of young people from around the nation who were brought to the same heartbreaking and permanent decision.

We must not forget these stories from our past. We must use them to teach ourselves and to illuminate a path to a future filled with endurance and resilience, which we all have within us. Let us be encouraged to rise above the poor behavior we see all around us and not let the poor behavior consume us. Rather, we must let it bring us to a place of compassion and mercy toward others, as well as, inward to ourselves. Let these stories take us to a future that calls us to be kind, caring, thoughtful, and respectful human beings in all the places and spaces we enter, including the digital cyber world. We should not run from the past or try to forget it but rather allow the past to give us hope for a better future, never letting these stories of children lost to bullying continue to be repeated.

Only after hearing and being moved by personal stories can we move forward to a place of empathy, trying to see the world through someone else's eyes. Understanding that we will never always agree with everyone all of the time, but that we must always continue to engage in respectful dialogue. We must always try to be good listeners, slowing down and actively hearing what others are saying, pausing, thinking, and choosing our words thoughtfully, carefully, and with respect before responding. Because words have great impact and do hurt if used as a weapon, as was the case for my son Tyler, as well as in many of the stories you will be reading in this book.

Using the stories from our past can help to motivate us to create a culture shift to one of kindness and empathy for everyone, not despite our differences but rather because our many differences should be respected and celebrated! What made Tyler different from his roommate was Tyler's sexual orientation. In my heart I believe that is why his roommate targeted and humiliated Tyler before his new dorm mates. He was trying to make Tyler feel broken, worthless, and less than, rather than celebrating this God-given trait that made Tyler special, precious, and unique. We all have talents and traits that make us unique and special, and I hope we can come to a place where we always see these differences as the true gifts that they were intended to be, worthy of acknowledgement, gratitude, and praise.

Stating a clear message of acceptance of everyone, not regardless, but rather because of what makes them unique, special, and precious, from the very beginning is an important strategy in preventing those painful scars that bullying causes. Imagine if every teacher, coach, or team captain stood up on the first day the group gathered and declared that it was not acceptable to humiliate or intimidate anyone in this space because of the color of their skin, where they came from, what language they spoke at home, how they dressed, their abilities or lack of abilities, whom they loved, what gender they identified as, or anything else that made them special, precious, or unique.

This is such a simple idea, but it is so very important for that marginalized or vulnerable child to hear. A message that they are welcome and included in this group and no one will be allowed to target them here! Such an important message for all of us to hear no matter our age! "You are cherished, you are safe, and we will protect you here, just as you are, perfectly created in God's image!" This is my hope for all to know, this simple truth and it is part of our core mission at the Tyler Clementi Foundation.

I do hope this book will inspire you to take action because everyone has the power and control to build a stronger, safer, more respectful and empathetic space wherever we are — at home, school, work, faith communities and especially in the digital world. This vision can be a reality if we all join together on this mission, changing one small corner of the world at a time!

Jane Clementi
Co-founder Tyler Clementi Foundation
www.tylerclementi.org

PREFACE

"Here she is again, turns up every summer like a bad penny!" I sang out as I entered the Minuteman Press on Falmouth Road strip mall in Centerville, Massachusetts.

"Not a bad penny, like a shiny penny," replied Sara immediately with her big, beautiful smile.

I could not believe how much her kind, spontaneous words touched me. I had just completed my chapter on the power of kindness, and this personal encounter underscored the importance of that message.

This book was written in response to a "call to action" by an editorial board, and in response to an untold number of people from all walks of life who spoke to me about the need for this book.

Although *Banishing Bullying Behavior: A Call to Action From Early Childhood Through Senior Adulthood* was intended to focus on workplace bullying, it quickly became obvious that workplace bullying does not take place in isolation but rather must be addressed in a continuum from early childhood through senior adulthood.

An estimated fifty percent of the students who bully at school are bullied at home either by a parent or siblings. The parents who are bullies at home probably take that behavior into the workplace as well.

The continuum of bullying behavior is discussed in great detail in the pages of this book based on the landmark Eron longitudinal study. They are brought to life by the many individuals who wanted to share their experiences with me so others could be spared the enormous pain they endured.

Their stories are shared using only a "new" first name and with a change of location to protect their identities. In some cases, the individuals were comfortable to have their full names used.

The book was ready "to be put to bed," and yet another individual came forward with yet another compelling story to be shared, a story that seemed to contain so many elements discussed in this book.

I was in Chicago for a professional meeting and decided to stay a few extra days to visit with family and friends. One friend who had moved from Kansas City many years ago hosted a dinner party for me to meet her "significant other" and close friends. Pretty early in the conversation my hostess mentioned that I was writing my third book on bullying, this one including workplace bullying, and one of the guests promptly spoke up, "I think you will find my workplace situation of interest." And indeed, it included so many elements covered in the chapters of this book.

Jill, mother of three teenagers and wife of a lawyer, has pursued a successful career in the not-for-profit world. She has been in her present position for six years, on a staff of nine, three full-time and six part-time, including Jill as part-time. The organization is twelve years old, very successful in its mission. Jill loves her work but said that the work environment under the leadership of its COO was very difficult.

"I have the utmost respect for my boss and her success but not for her leadership," Jill told me. "She is unpredictable and will lash out at staff members when least expected. Most of our staff members last only two or three years and then move on, some with serious health-related issues, often related to stress."

Jill's story includes so many aspects to be considered in workplace bullying:
- The importance of the job interview and considering employee revolving-door turnover as a red flag for a bully environment
- Professional leadership to create a positive work environment
- Addressing stress-related issues
- The reality of bully bosses who are retained in their jobs because of their enormous success

Jill seemed to bring together my years of interviews with people who had endured so much.

I invite you to respond to this call to action to learn from those who have been willing to share their experiences and to help to create an environment in which we can work to banish bullying behavior.

Chapter One

A CALL TO ACTION

Tyler Clementi grew up with a love for music and began playing the violin in the third grade. By the time he was eighteen and entered Rutgers University as a freshman, he had already been the recipient of several awards in recognition of his talent and his contribution to the world of music.

Tyler "came out" the summer before his freshman year in college. When he asked his dorm roommate for privacy one evening while he had a friend over, his roommate used a webcam to stream footage of Tyler in an intimate act. When Tyler learned through his roommate's Twitter feed that he had become "a topic of ridicule in his new environment," he committed suicide by jumping off the George Washington Bridge.

"What has been will be again, what has been done will be done again; there is nothing new under the sun."

— Ecclesiastes 1:19

That is certainly true with respect to bullying, which can be traced back to Biblical times. Until fairly recently bullying was considered a "rite of passage." "Boys will be boys." However, we now know all too well that bullying is not a rite of passage, but that it can span a lifetime from early childhood through senior adulthood.

The tragic death of the talented young Tyler Clementi (December 19, 1991-September 22, 2010) has served as a "call to action." Newspapers across the country and around the world are sounding a call to action to address the life-threatening consequences of bullying behavior. Such a call to action was sounded by the *Sioux City Journal* editorial board under the headline **"Our Opinion: We must stop bullying. It starts here. It starts now."**

"Siouxland lost a young life to a senseless, shameful tragedy last week. By all accounts Kenneth Weishuhn was a kind-hearted, fun-loving boy, always looking to make others smile. But when the South O'Brien High School fourteen-year-old told friends he was gay the harassment and bullying began. It didn't let up until he took his own life.

"Sadly, Kenneth's story is far from unique. Boys and girls across Iowa and beyond are targeted every day. In this case sexual orientation seems to have played a role, but we have learned a bully needs no reason to strike. No sense can be made of these actions. Now our community and region must face that stark reality. We are all to blame. We have not done enough. Not nearly enough."

This *Sioux City Journal* Opinion piece addresses a serious problem in communities, large and small, throughout our country and beyond. The editorial board stresses that this is not only a school problem, but in order to banish bullying behavior the whole community must be involved.

"We must make it clear in our actions and our words that bullying will not be tolerated. Those of us in public life must be ever mindful of the words we choose, especially in contentious political debates that have defined our modern times. More importantly we must not be afraid to act."

This outstanding opinion piece by the editorial board of the *Sioux City Journal* is a response to what has come before and tragically reflects what has happened since then. Yes, there have been responses to this impassioned call to action — this book is one such response. I wish I could say that this opinion piece has made a huge impact, stopping bullying in its tracks in Sioux City and beyond, but sadly, that is not the case. Much more is desperately needed. The lack of civility among our youth as well as adults seems to be getting worse instead of better in our country and around the world.

In addition to its resounding call to action this opinion piece demands that we ask ourselves some serious questions. How can we educate our students to understand that the Kenneth Weishuhns and Tyler Clementis of this world are the same likeable people after they "came out" as they were before they "came out" regardless of their sexual orientation? This is the twenty-first century; we must provide the scientific education so that students understand and respect differences in sexual orientation. They should be taught respect for differences among all people, regardless of race, creed, heritage, religion, and gender identity. Gay students are bullied three times as much as other students. This is unacceptable and must be addressed as part of age-appropriate curricula. With appropriate education hopefully we can spare future students the tragic fate experienced by so many of the young people you will meet in the pages of this book.

How do we address a fundamental flaw in our society that allows for bullying to take place? Certainly, one answer to that question is that we start in the home. Parenting is probably the most important "job" we have and yet the one many individuals are the least prepared for. Those individuals who are fortunate enough to grow up in homes filled with unconditional love *are* well prepared to do the same once they start their own families. However, respect and kindness are not taught and modeled in enough homes to eradicate this fundamental flaw in our society.

Education can perhaps provide what is not provided in many homes. A foundation for a loving home could be established by a mandatory high school course on parenting with an interactive curriculum that is taught by a dynamic instructor. This is a tall order, and its success will depend on both the curriculum and the instructor. Modeling kindness and respect must be an essential component of the course as they should be in all courses. For those who do not finish high school, this course could be provided by social service agencies, houses of worship, GED courses, or offered in the workplace. It would also be appropriate to offer these classes in prisons, especially for young offenders and those who are already parents.

Education is a great place to start, but no one course, or even several courses, will be enough to stop the cruelty on the school bus, on the playground, and on the Internet. The issue needs to be addressed on many fronts and will take the concerted effort of many people. Those who are working hardest to make a difference are likely the parents of young people whose lives have been lost to *bullycide* — suicide that occurs as the result of bullying.

Brenda High is one such parent. After losing her son Jared to bullycide she went to the frontlines of the battle against bullying and founded Bully Police USA, a watchdog organization advocating for bullied children and reporting on various states' anti-bullying laws. Thanks to Brenda and her organization, as of March 2015 all fifty states now have anti-bullying laws, the first having been passed by the Georgia legislature in 1995.

Bully Police USA evaluates the laws on ten criteria assigning a grade between A++ and D:

- A++ = Near perfect laws, include cyber bullying
- B = Acceptable laws
- C = Mediocre laws
- D = Worthless laws

The criteria include accountability, provision for counseling for victims, handling of lawsuits, and protection against reprisals, and they encourage states to mandate the establishment of anti-bullying laws rather than just suggest legislation.

I urge you to go to the Bully Police USA website, www.bullypolice.org. It has a wealth of information about bullycide prevention and also about the children whom have been lost to bullycide, including Brenda's son Jared, who was just thirteen when he took his life after years of being bullied. Brenda relates Jared's story in her book *Bullycide in America: Moms Speak Out About the Bullying/Suicide Connection* published in 2007, with a second edition in 2012. In this compelling book, six moms tell the heartbreaking stories of the loss of their children to bullycide in the hope that the lessons learned will spare other parents the lifelong grief of loss this devastating.

Jared's story is one that tragically has been repeated over and over again. He was a "typical" boy growing up in a loving home, targeted by bullies and assaulted by one bully. His parents made endless attempts to have the school administration intervene — to no avail. They had Jared change schools and finally were forced to take legal action against the school administration, but before the tide could be reversed the effects of bullying triggered depression in their son that ultimately led to bullycide.

On Brenda's Bully Police USA website, you can view a picture of a quilt made by Linda Hannawalt with 223 names of victims of bullycide to honor their memories and their lives. Her design focuses on each child's life and interests. These are all stories of young people whose lives irreversibly changed course due to the actions of a bully.

Although most school districts now have bully prevention programs in place as mandated by the states' legislatures (thanks to the work of Brenda High and Bully Police USA), the programs don't seem to be enough to prevent ongoing bullying behavior. The list of bullycides is growing daily, along with the list of grief-stricken families.

Another family that has turned its grief into action is the family of Tyler Clementi, who has established the Tyler Clementi Foundation. On the Foundation website Tyler's mother speaks not only for herself and her family but for the families of the hundreds of victims of bullycide.

"My son, Tyler, is the reason I, along with my husband Joseph and son James, have dedicated the last five years of our lives to sharing our personal tragedy with the world. The loss that we experienced in September 2010 devastated us and permanently transformed our family, our lives, and our purposes. We could not go back in time and change the choice Tyler made, even though it was the only thing I wanted; the only thing that would make me whole again. I have spent years learning to live with loss and pain, and it continues to be a learning process. The one thing I know is that no family should have to endure a tragedy like ours."

Through her work with the Foundation, Jane Clementi learned "just how widespread and rampant a problem bullying is in our culture." Many people have shared their stories with Jane Clementi, and she "found that Tyler's story had a universal quality that many people could relate to in some way."

I highly recommend that you go to the website, www.tylerclementi.org, to learn about the outstanding work the Foundation is doing. It will give you an opportunity to respond to the call for action.

Although many of the dramatic bullying stories that make the news happen to middle school through high school students, bullying starts much earlier than that. Preschools and elementary schools are also settings for peer abuse. One father, whose six-year-old daughter was bullied in a Wisconsin elementary school by a five-year-old classmate, was forced to file a temporary restraining order as a last resort. Even though the five-year-old bully had admitted to the school principal that he'd said to his victim, "I want to slit your throat and watch it bleed," she told the father that "he didn't mean it." The father had also pointed out that the bully pushed his daughter around on the playground and threw rocks at her during recess. Only after the paperwork for the restraining order was filed did the school officials decide they should take action.

The young target in this story is not the only one who needed help and protection. Clearly the words uttered by the bully were a serious cry for help: one has to wonder where a five-year-old might hear such phrases. Bullying behavior such as this requires immediate intervention — for the welfare of both the target and the bully.

If it goes unchecked, bullying behavior will continue into the higher grades and well beyond. Peer abuse occurs in retirement communities as well as in the schoolyard. The vast majority of senior adult bullies have been bullies since childhood.

Not only is bullying found in every age group, it is also found in every setting — home, school, the workplace, senior centers, and more. And workplace bullying is not particular to any one field over another. It occurs in fields as diverse as the medical profession, the legal profession, academia, sports, and minimum wage jobs.

As I conducted interviews for this book, physicians told me that they thought bullying in the medical profession is "the worst," lawyers told me that they thought bullying in the legal profession is "the worst," and those in academia claimed that it is "the worst!"

When bullying behavior shows up in school-age children, it is estimated that fifty percent of these bullies are bullied at home, either by parents or siblings. And one can imagine that the parents who bully at home also might bully at the workplace. Bullying is not an isolated behavior, but rather a web of hurt being spun and passed along.

The call for action is thus not only to protect our children. It must reach far and wide, into all age groups and all settings. Bullying must not be tolerated anywhere, including among adults in the workplace. As the study of bullying deepens, new types of bullying are being identified. Those in positions of authority — whether teachers or school administrators or Human Resources in the workplace — must be alert to new forms of bullying that might crop up in unexpected ways.

Tim Field, who worked on the UK National Workplace Bullying Advice Line, identified the "serial bully" who bullies one individual until the victim can't take it anymore and then changes schools or jobs. Then the serial bully targets another individual until that victim can't take it anymore and also moves on. This bully only targets one person at a time and continues to torment that individual until he or she moves on.

Another type of bully has been identified as the "vicarious bully" — one who instigates a conflict between two other people or instructs one person to bully another. Being a bully is bad enough, but to have to do it for someone else seems strange, indeed.

It is important to remember that there has been an evolution in the vocabulary used to describe bullying behavior as more and more awareness is raised about the scope of the problem. Initially the term *victim* was universally used to describe the individual being attacked by the bully. The term *victim* has now evolved to *target*, with the idea that "victim" describes someone who has already been victimized while "target" indicates the potential ability to deflect the bully's attack.

Bullying is now often referred to as peer abuse or elder abuse that puts it into the context of other forms of abuse. This has underscored the fact that bullying is no longer to be considered "a rite of passage" for the victim and can cause harm that might last a lifetime.

The term *bystander* has been broadened to *witness*, again recognizing the ability to act and not just be passive during the bullying interaction. A witness might actually become a defender.

These terms have evolved from bullying in early childhood through senior adulthood. They reflect the progress that has been made in the battle against bullying, but we still have a long way to go.

The "unprecedented 2016 presidential campaign and election" put bullying behavior front and center. Teachers across the country reported the impact that it had on their students and in their classrooms. Only time will tell what the full impact of a bully in the White House will have on our country. Much is already being written about it on a daily basis. All the more reason that this "call to action" is so important.

Chapter Two

BULLYING CONTINUUM FROM EARLY CHILDHOOD THROUGH SENIOR ADULTHOOD

More than half a century ago, Leonard Eron, Ph.D., and his colleagues pioneered research on aggression with their landmark Columbia County Longitudinal Study (1960). This research has covered a forty-year span with the collection of four waves of data, thus far.

All the third graders in Columbia County, New York, participated in the study; 456 boys and 420 girls, as well as many of their parents, family members and teachers. The students were asked to check off the names of classmates they thought were bullies. The forms were collected and stored for a decade.

Ten years later, when the same students were seniors in high school, Dr. Eron and his colleagues repeated the process. Most of the students who had been identified by their classmates as bullies in the third grade were again checked off as bullies ten years later.

In the next wave of data collection, the researchers found that one out of every four students identified by their classmates in third grade as bullies had a criminal record by the age of twenty-eight to thirty. They found that male bullies often became abusive husbands and the females, abusive mothers. By contrast, non-bullying children appeared to have a one-in-twenty chance of becoming criminals as adults.

In addition to serious criminal problems, the individuals identified as bullies in third grade have gone on to have mental health issues, problems with substance abuse, and troubles at work. The cycle then continued with the children of these people being more likely to be identified by their classmates as bullies in third grade as well.

Bullycide in America: Moms Speak Out About the Bullying/Suicide Connection is a book in which seven moms tell the heartbreaking stories of how unbearable bullying led to their children's suicide. The book was compiled by Brenda High in 2007 to build awareness about how serious bullying is with the hope that education about this topic would prevent future tragedies.

Brandon Chris Swartwood's (February 21, 1982-December 16, 2000) story as told by his mom Cathy Swartwood Mitchell, chronicles years of torture by a group of bullies, the school's total failure to intervene, and the family's inability to get proper legal help. She believes that Brandon was one of several targets because the bullies were jealous of his good looks, intelligence, and other characteristics they would never be able to attain.

Cathy had researched the statistics, probably the work of Dr. Eron, and "knew what kind of men they would become." For many years she followed their court records and found that at least three of the perpetrators had numerous felony charges or convictions for some of their crimes. All three had some protective orders filed against them by their spouses or girlfriends. Other charges include possession of a controlled substance, multiple burglaries, domestic abuse, and child abuse.

Cathy concludes, "As students, they were liars, thieves, thugs, and abusers. Now these school bullies, in adulthood, they are societies' criminals."

From the Columbia County Longitudinal Study, it is clear that bullying isn't just a phase. Children and teens don't grow out of being bullies simply because they complete elementary school. It is also clear that bullying doesn't arise out of thin air; an estimated fifty percent of school bullies are bullied at home by either parents or siblings. Bullying is a continuum from childhood through the rest of life, and it is passed from one generation to the next. The only way to break the cycle is by recognizing it and addressing it with hands-on intervention. In order to do so, it is crucial to understand

and identify bullying in all stages of the life-long continuum and in a wide variety of settings.

As mentioned earlier, for many generations bullying was considered a "rite of passage," the province of schoolyard activities. "Hot spots" have always included the school bus, the lunchroom, the boys' and girls' restrooms, gym locker rooms, and any other venue the bullies could find to torture their victims.

Jena rode the school bus in her rural farm school district. She was the first one picked up in the morning and the last one dropped off in the afternoon. She also became the victim of ongoing bully and had no idea why.

Decades later Maryann accepted a job as a receptionist in a residential psychiatric center. One day a woman resident approached her and said, "Maryann, you don't recognize me, do you? I am Jena! Look where I ended up. Look at your life and look at mine!"

Maryann, in fact, did not recognize Jena and was overcome with bystander guilt and remorse. Although she had not done any of the bullying, she had not done anything to try to stop it; she had never even reported the daily torture directed at her classmate.

Later in this book you will meet a sixth-grade student who was the victim of such a horrific lunchroom bullying attack that he had to be hospitalized for five days.

Brandon was also so severely assaulted in the lunchroom that he required surgery. Lunchroom bullying is not limited to school lunchrooms; it happens in the workplace and senior adult facilities as well.

The boys' and girls' restrooms are notorious "hot spots" for bullying behavior. In one school, a savvy school security guard kept a keen eye peeled on the boys' restroom used by one of the school bullies. Whenever the guard saw the bully enter the restroom, he followed and busied himself with some housekeeping chore. What a wonderful example of intervention and prevention!

The gym locker rooms are also infamous on the list of "hot spots." Sally, now in her mid-fifties, told me about the pain she endured during middle school in the gym locker room. Her classmates' verbal bullying was relentless simply because her body had not matured as quickly as theirs; this, in spite of the fact that she was pretty and a good athlete.

Professionals in the field of education, especially school administrators, simply "looked the other way" when bullying occurred on their watch. As we read the heart-wrenching stories by the moms of the teens who committed bullycide at the end of the twentieth century, one common thread is the lack of help and support for victims of bullies and their families. It is the *response* to this situation by the families who lost children to bullycide that has had a significant impact on the leadership administrators are taking now to create bully-free zones in their schools.

EARLY CHILDHOOD

The continuum of bullying behavior can be observed at a very early age. During early childhood, from birth through five years of age, some children can be aggressive, domineering, and bossy. The aggressive child will grab a toy another child is playing with and refuse to return it when asked to do so. He might knock a child off a tricycle during preschool recess time on the playground, get on the trike, and ride off. The domineering preschool children will insist on having his or her way all the time and never take turns. The bossy child will constantly tell his/her peers what to do, when to do it, and how it should be done. Without appropriate intervention the aggressive preschooler will become the physical bully; the domineering and bossy youngsters will use verbal bullying on their targets.

Early childhood is when preschoolers learn how to share, take turns, play alone, and play with peers. With talented early childhood teachers, it is amazing to see how quickly young children learn these skills. The aggressive, domineering, and bossy children are few and far between, but they do "stick out like a sore thumb." As mentioned earlier they require immediate intervention, and if that intervention is not successful, they will be bullies as they move through the continuum.

These children often come from homes where they have little or no parental supervision, have not been taught appropriate social skills or are subjected to severe physical punishment.

SuEllen Fried and I discuss guidelines in detail for teachers' meetings with parents of bullies in our book, *Banishing Bullying Behavior: Transforming the Culture of Pain, Rage, and Revenge.* We encourage teachers to try to establish a partnership with parents, working together for the benefit of the child. Even abusive parents want what is best for their children.

An urgent wake-up call for parents and educators was sounded a number of years ago by Dorothy L. Espelage, Ph.D., in her publications and presentations: "In the fifteen years that I have studied bullying and other forms of youth aggression, the children have gotten younger and younger in the manifestations of their behaviors. The behaviors we saw in fifth-graders, we are now seeing in preschool playgroups. I think this is due in part to the introduction of technology to youth and their level of sophistication associated with their level of targeting each other."

It is amazing to learn that in just fifteen years aggressive youth behavior can have moved for fifth-graders to such young children. This makes modeling and teaching kindness as part of early childhood education all the more important.

ELEMENTARY SCHOOL

The continuum of bullying behavior can be observed throughout elementary school, ages six through twelve. In kindergarten and the early elementary grades, bullying looks similar to the behaviors that manifest in early childhood. A very popular form of bullying at this age is exclusion, telling classmates, "You can't play with us," during recess. An in-depth discussion of bullying during these years is included in the description of the Student Empowerment Session, later in this chapter.

Professor Aletha Huston is considered to be one of the experts in the area of child development during middle childhood (from ages nine to twelve). She and Marika Ripke, Ph.D., editors of the book *Developmental Contexts in Middle Childhood: Bridges to Adolescence and Adulthood,* conclude that "although lasting individual differences are evident by the end of the preschool years a child's developmental path in middle school childhood contributes significantly to the adolescent that he or she becomes."

Huston and Ripke continue by pointing out that this path forward goes beyond book learning. It is the ability to do the things we simply assume children are able to do at that age, like riding a bike, learning to swim and making friends. They stress that making friends is considered to be one of the most important tasks at this stage in children's lives. It is the time when they should be able to learn how to build healthy, rewarding peer relationships. As we all know, making friends and getting along with peers is a very important life skill that must be learned at this age.

It is during this period that children start to think abstractly, a key factor in the development of their reading skills and higher-level thinking. It is the age where students move from learning to read to reading to learn, from concrete thinking to abstract thinking. It is very important for parents and educators to challenge all children to reach their potential and to experience success both academically and socially. Normal development in these areas helps children to also develop a healthy sense of self-esteem that in turn serves as a powerful antidote to becoming a target of bullying.

Dr. Eron and his research team in the Columbia County Longitudinal Study starting with third grade students give us resounding evidence of significant consequences of bullying behavior at this age. It is imperative that bullies receive professional help in order to avoid the lifelong consequences that would otherwise lie ahead for them.

SIBLING ABUSE/BULLYING

There is growing recognition that the serious problem of sibling abuse or bullying has been overlooked far too long. With the rise in the number of blended families, the bullying of stepbrothers and stepsisters is also increasing. Each year nineteen million children are abused in their homes by their own siblings. Nearly two million children use weapons as a means of resolving a physical problem with a sibling. Ten percent of the murders in American families are committed by siblings of the victims. These staggering statistics underscore the critical need to address this problem. The problem, of course, does not stop when the targeted child leaves the home; many of these children who are bullied at home by siblings and/or parents commit much of the peer abuse that occurs at school.

MIDDLE SCHOOL BULLYING

There is ample research to indicate that bullying is at its worst among middle school students, between the ages of twelve and fourteen. The American Academy of Child and Adolescent Psychiatry states "this stage is a time of experimentation, testing limits, and a struggle for a sense of identity. These students' intellectual interests expand but at this age have limited thoughts of the future. They are awkward about their changing bodies and have an increased interest in sex. The taunting can be outrageous and relentless. Sexual bullying, especially around sexual language, is rampant and causes enormous pain."

Many of the targets and victims you will meet throughout the book were in middle school at the time they were bullied. For some, the bullying was just a continuation of earlier bullying; others suddenly became targets in middle school.

Adults, teachers and parents, are urged first and foremost to keep their middle school students and children safe. The abundant number of stories reported about the tyranny that takes place in middle schools around the country underscores the importance of adult vigilance and protection.

Many children are afraid to report bullying episodes for fear of being considered a snitch or tattletale. They should be taught the difference between tattling and reporting. Tattling on someone is to get them into trouble; reporting is telling a trusted adult about someone in order to get them out of trouble.

Many classrooms have mailboxes and/or internet options where students can report bullying episodes anonymously. This enables the students to take positive action and adults to intervene.

HIGH SCHOOL BULLYING

There is general agreement among the findings of numerous studies that between twenty and forty percent of U.S. teenagers report being bullied during the last number of years. Between seven and fifteen percent report bullying others three or more times during the last year.

According to professional observers of teen-age behavior, bullies are more likely than non-bullying teens to:
- Have difficulty accepting criticism
- Have the need to be the center of attention and will try to get it any way they can
- Drink alcohol and use drugs excessively
- Be at greater risk of being victimized themselves (about fifty percent of bullies are also victims at some point)

- Be at greater risk of mental health problems such as conduct disorder and attention deficit hyperactivity disorder
- Be antisocial in adulthood
- Use violence in relationships
- Get into trouble with law

On the other side of the coin, the targets are more likely than non-bullied teens to:
- Be at higher risk for mental and physical health problems such as depression, stomachaches, and headaches
- Be absent from school more frequently because of fear of being bullied
- Continue to experience higher levels of anxiety through adulthood
- Have low self-worth
- Feel that they are not in control of their lives

Debbie Wilborn was at the forefront of these observations that she reported in 2008. Since that time, these characteristics continue to be observed by professionals, which enables them to address the issues they raise and intervene on behalf of both bullies and targets.

TEENAGE DATING ABUSE

Phyllis told me that she really had not noticed that her daughter, Margo, was wearing long-sleeved, high-neck tops and was no longer wearing mini-skirts. Instead she was wearing pants and tights. She did observe that Margo and her boyfriend, Chris, didn't spend any time with the family and their high school friends, something they had done earlier in their relationship. It was only when she chanced upon an article that included the following information that she realized that Margo might be in an abusive relationship.

It took Phyllis some time to get Margo to admit that the change in attire was to hide ongoing bruising inflicted by Chris as he became more and more possessive of Margo's undivided attention. As the following statistics indicate, Margo's dating abuse is quite prevalent. Margo required extensive professional counseling to extricate herself from the abusive relationship and to begin to heal emotionally.

A key component of high school bullying is dating abuse. The National Teen Dating Abuse Hotline and many similar agencies report the following:
- One in five teens who have been in a serious relationship reports being hit, slapped, or shoved by a partner.
- One in three girls who have been in a serious relationship says she has been concerned about being physically hurt by her partner.
- One in four teens who have been in a serious relationship says his/her boyfriend or girlfriend has tried to prevent him/her from spending time with friends or family; the same number has been pressured to only spend time with his/her partner.
- One in three girls between the ages of sixteen and eighteen says sex is expected for people her age if she is in a relationship; half of the teen girls who have experienced sexual pressure report they are afraid the relationship would break up if they did not give in.
- Nearly one in four girls (twenty-three percent) reported going further sexually than they wanted to as a result of pressure.

ADULT BULLYING

Bullying does not end with childhood; unfortunately, it is rampant in adulthood. It can be found in the home and the workplace. Bullying in the workplace will be discussed in great detail in Chapters Six and Seven.

SENIOR CITIZEN BULLYING

An estimated ten to twenty percent of senior citizens living in retirement centers and other senior facilities are reported to be targets or victims of bullies. When there is no hands-on intervention early in the continuum, bullies continue their bullying behavior all the way into senior adulthood. In addition, we see new bullies emerge among those individuals who feel a loss of control or power they exerted earlier in life in family and business matters and no longer possess. Now they are trying to regain a feeling of control or to exert power over a likely target in their new surroundings.

Many of the same types of bullying behavior that occur all along the continuum are played out in senior adulthood as well. The most common form of bullying at this stage in life is emotional, such as spreading rumors, and exclusion, especially at meals.

Once again, we see so many of those symptoms experienced by targets and victims all along the bullying continuum: anxiety, depression, elevated blood pressure, fatigue, increased isolation, feelings of rejection, and lower self-esteem. Attempted suicides also have been reported, just as we see among children and teen targets and victims.

No matter the age, as young as early childhood or as old as senior adulthood, the pain inflicted by bullying has lasting effects. The number of adults who asked me to interview them to share their bullying experiences from decades earlier amazes me. In many interviews it was obviously painful but cathartic; in others it was clear that the victims hoped sharing their experiences could spare others their pain.

THE STUDENT EMPOWERMENT SESSION

Many powerful definitions of types of bullying have come from K-12 students during Student Empowerment Sessions (SES) [1], a program developed by SuEllen Fried almost two decades ago. Since then, Fried has implemented the SES program with over 60,000 students in thirty-six states.

After reading about Fried's SES I asked her if she would demonstrate it for one of my undergraduate education classes. I arranged to have Fried conduct the session for three sections of sixth-graders in a local public school. The sixty sixth-graders sat on the floor of the all-purpose room, and my students sat on the floor in the back of the room and observed. The classroom teachers also observed the session. Fried opened the session by introducing herself and sharing the true story about ten-year old Kim, who had cancer and was bullied on the playground by boys who pulled off her wig and made fun of her bald head. Fried told the story in a way that every child in the room could relate to Kim; you could hear a pin drop.

She then explained that she would like to learn more about bullying from them. Fried stresses that using the Socratic method of asking

---

[1] *The SES program is described in detail in the book SuEllen Fried and I co-authored, Banishing Bullying Behavior: Transforming the Culture of Peer Abuse. The chapter titled "Empowering Students in the Solution" was designed to guide educators and school counselors in conducting these sessions.*

questions is an absolutely essential part of the process. All questions should be open-ended and allow for a multitude of answers.

The questions should be presented in a particular order. Each session lasts about an hour, with some forty to sixty students participating, all from the same grade level.

The following descriptions of the types of bullying are a composite of student responses to Student Empowerment Sessions:

PHYSICAL BULLYING

When students are asked to define physical bullying during Student Empowerment Sessions they literally shout out dozens of examples, such as the obvious poking, shoving, hitting, tripping, and punching as well as the less frequent instances of urinating on someone, swirly (forcing someone's head into the toilet and flushing the toilet, a favorite in the boys' restroom), shooting, and stabbing. Any type of physical contact that can be hurtful and inflict pain is classified as physical bullying.

VERBAL BULLYING

Verbal bullying includes any use of words to hurt the intended target. In her book *Bullies and Victims,* Fried asked students to change the well-known sticks-and-stones phrase to: "Sticks and stones can break your bones, but words can break your heart." During discussions about verbal bullying, students and adults talk about the fact that broken bones usually heal in a matter of weeks or months, but broken hearts may never heal.

A few examples of verbal bullying include spreading rumors, sarcasm, mimicking, whispering, making fun of disabilities, and put-downs.

EMOTIONAL BULLYING

Emotional bullying is non-verbal forms of aggression such as pointing, staring, exclusion, rejection, ostracizing, or turning your back on someone. Child advocate Dorothy Dean has stated "emotional abuse is the most difficult type of abuse to define and diagnose. Physical abuse, verbal abuse, and some sexual abuse can be documented and verified. The target, if old enough, can describe what occurred. Emotional abuse, however, is intangible. The wounds are internal, but they may be more devastating and crippling than other forms of abuse."

Tanya, who spoke so softly I had to strain to hear her, shared a poignant example of emotional bullying. "No one ever invited me to their birthday parties, so when my birthday came along, I sent an invitation to everyone in my class. My mom and I baked cupcakes for everyone, and we put their names on with icing. We got gift bags for everyone and we planned some special games. It was going to be the best birthday I ever had. On the day of my party, I waited and waited and waited, but no one came."

Exclusion is one of the most painful forms of bullying — from early childhood, where students in preschool may not allow a classmate to join their play group — to students in middle school getting up from the lunchroom table when a target comes to sit down, and it goes all through adolescence and beyond. Unfortunately, this exclusion behavior does not stop just because grade school ends. The same behavior shows up in the workplace, as illustrated in the widely reported Miami Dolphins scandal, where teammates got up from the lunch table when Jonathan Martin tried to join them. Even in the continuum of bullying among senior citizens living in retirement communities, bullies sometimes don't allow their targets to join them at meals.

Following the discussion of the types of bullying Fried moved to a discussion of sympathy, empathy, and apologies, which had to be more than "I am sorry," but were a promise that the behavior would not be repeated. She then asked if there was anyone brave enough to make an apology. Several hands went up, and apologies were made, even two going back to kindergarten! The students were asked if they accepted the apologies, and all responses were affirmative.

Needless to say, it was a very inspiring and informative session. As we were leaving the school, I told Fried how impressed I was but didn't think I could get the same results she did. Her response was, "Yes, you will! The pain is so close to the surface for these children, they welcome the opportunity to talk about it."

Just a few weeks later I conducted a session in another school for sixty fifth-graders, and as Fried predicted, I had the same results. A year later I was working with some interns in the same school and had the opportunity to ask the principal whether he thought the impact of the session carried over through the year. He assured me that it had.

WHAT CAN BE DONE?

There is general agreement that peer abuse no longer is solely the province of the schoolyard and school bus. *It has become clear that bullying occurs at all ages from early childhood through the lives of senior citizens.* It takes place at home by parents and siblings, at school by classmates and adults, and in the workplace at all levels.

Cyber bullying follows its targets from school and the workplace into the home with unfathomable cruelty that is hard to escape. The serious consequences of cyber bullying make devastating headlines throughout the country, in small towns and large cities, in rural areas and in the urban core across all socioeconomic levels of society.

The cycle of this behavior, in many cases passed from parent to child and then on to the next generation, is one that needs to be broken. And it must be broken in the home, at school, in the workplace and beyond. Change is certainly difficult to bring about, but it is interesting to note how some of the changes we see taking place started. Who asked their parents to stop smoking? Who insists that seat belts be used? Who is raising awareness about environmental issues and recycling? In many cases the answer is the youth in our society.

Some of the credit for this change has come as the result of children learning about the health hazard of smoking in school and asking their parents to stop smoking. The Centers for Disease Control and Prevention reports adult smoking today is at the lowest since reporting started in 1965, with statistics indicating downward movement in recent years. We still have a long way to go, but we are moving in the right direction.

How often do children insist that their parents and grandparents "buckle up?"

The National Highway Traffic Safety Administration survey reported a two-percent increase in use of seat belts in one year. Many factors are credited for this move in the right direction, and children should be included.

I have been enormously heartened by observing student leadership in the "going green" movement in schools. Students are doing an excellent job of getting their peers to recycle. These same students are encouraging their parents to recycle at home.

Let us hope that with education and adult leadership our youth will have the same influence to change bullying behavior. We must bring about change in the level of civility and kindness in the lives of all children and adults through their senior years.

Chapter Three

"ONCE A BULLY, ALWAYS A BULLY..."

Annie is a doctoral student researching the lack of civility in the workplace among coworkers and between customers and sales personnel. She is also a manager in a very large financial company located in the northeastern United States.

Eight years ago, when she was a new, young employee, she was bullied by her supervisor for well over a year. "She bullied the heck out of me," Annie confided. "No one goes into the workplace prepared for that kind of treatment by one's boss." Annie was shocked by the frequency and intensity of the behavior. Only with experience did she realize that her boss's behavior was rooted in her own insecurity. The outward expression of it was a need to be in control and a belief that no one could do any job as well as she could.

"My life was hell until I finally went to Human Resources," Annie said. She was transferred to work under a different supervisor. "HR was very effective in bringing about a resolution to the problem by intervening quickly and making it clear that such behavior would not be tolerated."

Ironically, a number of years later Annie was accused of bullying by three employees under her supervision. Given her previous experience, she was shocked by the accusation and tried her best to rectify the situation. She met individually with each employee, as well as with them as a group, but to no avail. She was not able to ascertain what in her behavior had given them the impression that she was bullying them. To this day, all these many years later, she still does not know what prompted these isolated accusations. She certainly had no intention of bullying anyone and asked Human Resources to transfer the individuals to another department.

We are left wondering whether this is just a matter of poor chemistry between employees and their supervisor or whether it could be reverse bullying.

Annie's experience underscores the complex nature of the workplace environment.

During our lengthy interview, Annie blurted out, "Once a bully, always a bully." I was surprised by how vehemently she'd said this and asked if she really meant to be as emphatic as she made it sound. She then repeated, "Once a bully, always a bully . . . unless there's a spiritual experience." Indeed, a spiritual awakening is a unique and profound experience and can change a person fundamentally; perhaps you know this firsthand from your own life or that of a loved one. Another person I interviewed, who I knew could relate to this, was Andrew Bash. I shared Annie's words with Andrew because I knew they would resonate with him.

"That statement gave me goose bumps," he said. "I'm not sure anyone can have a lasting transformation without some kind of spiritual influence. I agree one hundred percent."

Andrew has been on a spiritual journey for the fourteen years he has been a "recovering bully." When he learned, just by chance, that I was working on this book, he asked to meet with me so he could share his story, with the hope it would spare others the pain he experienced as a bully.

Andrew started to bully "big time" in second grade when his parents were going through a divorce. He continued being a bully until he was thirty years old. Andrew maintains that he behaved that way because of a need to feel in control where he did not have any. "My inside voice told me that I was no good. I then acted externally how I was feeling inside." In retrospect Andrew believes that subconsciously he felt that by inflicting pain on others it would somehow lessen the enormous pain he was feeling throughout his school years, into college, and beyond. Ultimately this inner pain led to alcoholism and drug abuse. "The irony of me becoming an alcoholic,"

Andrew said, "is that without becoming an alcoholic and making the decision to spend more time hurting myself through booze and drugs and less time hurting others, I never would have had the spiritual experience necessary to transform."

Andrew is a highly successful, respected forty-four-year-old businessman in Kansas City. He is the father of three elementary-age children, determined to do whatever is necessary to create bully-free classrooms for them and others.

WHAT PROMPTS A FORMER BULLY TO TELL HIS STORY?[2]

"I really want people to connect with the sadness that's going on inside of the bully. I also want to make sure that the sadness does not excuse the behavior."

Andrew shares his story about decades of bullying behavior, which lasted well into adulthood, in order to help people understand that those who are bullied are not the only ones who feel pain. The bullies themselves also experience a tremendous amount of psychological and even physical pain. His aim is to educate and to impress upon people the importance of early intervention.

Andrew now realizes that he was a bully from about the second grade through college and as an adult as well. He was large for his age, intimidating just by his size. His harshest bullying came through using words that made people feel uncomfortable. However, he did use both physical and verbal abuse as means of bullying.

He was about nine or ten when his parents divorced. It was a stressful divorce, and this stress at home helped add to his own insecurity, which by then was already in place. The insecurity increased as he grew older. Many people find it surprising to learn that some bullies are insecure, but it is precisely this insecurity that the bullies try to "cover up" or hide by being a bully.

---

[2] *This chapter is based on two interviews with Andrew, one conducted by Sylvia LaVine for a publicity release and one with me to discuss opportunities for Andrew to make presentations to children of all ages, as well as to adults. It also is based on material he has written for these presentations.*

His parents were aware of what was going on, but the divorce made it difficult for them to present a unified front and therefore unable to properly address his bullying behavior. Recently, when Andrew spoke to his mother about his bullying behavior, she was in complete denial of the fact that he had ever been a bully, in spite of the fact that he is sure she was aware of it when it was going on!

"In third through sixth grade I started hanging out with several other kids whose parents were divorced. Even though we weren't able to articulate our feelings at that age, there was a sort of pact because you knew who those kids were, the ones who went to a different house on the weekends. I was with my dad on Wednesdays and every other weekend. My dad was good at making money and then throwing it at certain situations," Andrew said.

Andrew was always able to sense people who were weaker or had weaknesses, and he was incredibly good at manipulation, an Eddie Haskell kind of guy. Parents liked him because, like so many bullies, he could be charming when he wanted to be ... with teachers and other adults as well. All through school he made decent grades, Bs and Cs, without studying or really making any effort. Initially he wasn't a leader on the playground.

Andrew started drinking and playing football at fourteen. He was still running with the guys whose parents were divorced. He felt that they had a "commonality." He was fairly popular in junior high and definitely in high school. As is often the case with bullies, people would rather be nice to them for fear that if they get on their "bad side" they would become targets. He continued to inflict both physical and verbal abuse. He even got beaten up by some people whom he had pushed to the brink, people that he had been horrible to, time and time again. In the seventh grade he got into a fight with a guy who split his lip.

Andrew pointed out that, "The perpetrator was one year older and having a tough time. He was decent looking, just a kid who didn't fit in with a group. And I joined in and amplified that."

The bullying intensified in high school. Andrew had fewer inhibitions about being inappropriate. At parties he'd pick on people, throw his weight around. He was popular with girls, and he had several people who wanted to stay on his good side. He used to say, "For every enemy I make, I am able to make two friends." Today these people are called "lieutenants."

He remembers saying that he would harass someone and would get laughs. He had a following, even more so when he got into athletics. He was a football player and had become a leader on and off the field.

"I think this is what my bullying expressed: I wanted acceptance, I wanted validation, and I wanted to *eliminate anything* that was threatening to me, *anybody* who was threatening to me. Even though I now recognize the fact that I probably identified with these people more than I was aware of. But bullying was a way to hide my weaknesses. So, instead of saying to these (victims), 'I don't fit in either,' I would bully them."

Andrew's insight as an adult gives us a valuable opportunity to learn about what drives some bullies to act as they do. The need for acceptance and strong feelings of insecurity appear to play an important role in the lives of young bullies. It is extremely important to consider bullying behavior as "a call for help" and to get professional intervention for the bully. Parents, teachers and workplace managers must understand that bullying behavior is a symptom of some potentially serious problems and find a way to address them by getting appropriate professional help.

COLLEGE

When Andrew went to college where he didn't know anybody, he felt that it was an opportunity to leave his past behind and begin a new chapter in his life. He was overweight when he went to Indiana. He'd played football in high school, planned on playing football at college, and had been invited to be a 'walk on' for football. He had taken a round of steroids to be sure he was strong enough. Then he broke his hand on somebody's head right before he left Kansas City in yet another bullying incident. So, he stopped working out and got kind of soft. He joined a fraternity and started drinking too much. Drunk, he went to a game, got into a fight, and "then some kid beat the daylights out of me." At this point he weighed about 265 pounds and was six-foot-three.

Andrew found himself at college no longer the person he had been, no longer the big shot and the athlete. In college it was all about being attractive and smart rather than being the "big guy." So, the rules changed.

Sometimes when he came back to Kansas City, he was still a bully. But in college, at this point, alcohol and drugs became a more significant part of his life. He believes this was a sort of escape.

"But then bullying is somewhat of an escape as well. You're trying to get outside of your head. You're going outside to fix the inside, without having to pay any attention to the inside," Andrew told me.

Second semester of his sophomore year, Andrew was trying to get into business school. Discussions about his drinking first took place when he lived in the fraternity house. Andrew maintained that he was intelligent enough to know that he needed to move out of the fraternity house to study.

The night before the big meeting for new members of the business school, Andrew went drinking with a bunch of friends. They were joking about the fact that if you missed the meeting, you didn't get into business school. Unfortunately, he missed the meeting and never was accepted into business school.

However, a professor did let him take courses in the Business School, but he was not allowed to take any of the 'A Core' classes (the ones that led to a business degree).

At Christmas when he came home, he got into a fight with his father and his stepmother and told them that he didn't need their money anymore.

He waited tables at Red Lobster and drank all the time. Andrew was still in the fraternity but never returned to live in the house. The fraternity had many discussions with him about his drinking. Andrew knew that "when you're in the fraternity known as the 'Party House' and they want to talk to you about your drinking . . . that means that you probably aren't doing too well! So, what does all this mean? It goes back to the old escape thing and the insecurities and the inability to just be who I am and being comfortable being who I am."

Again, this underscores what drives so many people, young and old, to bully: their need to escape, their insecurities, and in many cases a need to control. In most cases it takes professional intervention to get to the root cause for the bullying behavior. School counselors in many cases have the appropriate credentials and if further help is needed should make the necessary referrals. Human Resources personnel should also have the equally appropriate training and know when referrals are necessary for additional intervention.

THE EPIPHANY

Andrew does admit that part of his change, his epiphany, did come from doing drugs, *which he does not recommend!* He believes that the hallucinogenic, the acid, the mushrooms did give him a certain insight. It did change him, but not enough to *stop* doing drugs and alcohol. He went from being a bully to a borderline Buddhist. But none of it is who you really are. It is just that he identified with something that made more sense than the last thing he was doing. He didn't know what the goal was and still felt lost.

Fast forward. Andrew is thirty years old, living in LA. In 1999, he had eleven W2s for total earnings of maybe $16,000, which meant he had eleven different jobs in one year. He had graduated from MU (University of Missouri) and gone into the insurance business and then banking and then moved to LA. His goal was to sign bands to a record label and then get into the music business. Even in those days he had a lot of his friends' parents who were like "my fans." They understood that his home situation was screwed up, and they gave him a lot of slack. Some of these adults were concerned about the fact that Andrew no longer had any contact with his father and stepmother at a time in his life when a positive father-son relationship was very important. Many of them never saw the bully side of Andrew and responded to his very likeable personality. Andrew personifies the two sides of many bullies, young and old. They are able to hide their insecurities behind a charming façade.

Then Andrew started attending Alcoholics Anonymous meetings. He found getting sober to be an eye-opener when you stop drugs and drinking to escape and finally have to face who you are. Then you do the Twelve Steps, and in the Steps you do your "inventory," which is the Fourth Step. You basically make a list of your resentments, of anyone you resent. You turn that list inside out and ask what your part was in each resentment. Andrew found that he had a lot of names on the inventory list! That exercise was what truly helped him to get a start on understanding who he is.

You survey this list of resentments, and as you break it into parts, you see how your part in each incident affected the other person. The Ninth Step of the AA program is that you are required to make amends with these people. Amends are not apologies. Amends are acts of contrition in which you say more than "I'm sorry." You actually ask what you can do to make the situation better.

"You don't know when you are young and a bully, you don't know how significant a moment in time can be for your victim. And how important an act of forgiveness can be when it is given to the bully. Let me tell you a story about the effect making amends can have," Andrew said.

"I was standing at an open house in Mission Hills. I am now a realtor, married, living in Kansas City. A guy walks in, we're talking, and he looks at me as if he wants to punch me. His energy is terribly aggressive. He looks at me, and then he says, 'I know who you are. Do you remember me?' I said no, and he said, 'You used to make fun of my last name all the time. You and your friends named a cat after my brother.' He wasn't asking for a fight, but he definitely meant to be clear about the pain I had caused him in high school. I told him that I couldn't discuss this with him here but asked him if he would be willing to meet for coffee. I wanted time to think about this, and I wanted to make amends. I kind of remembered a party where I gave him a really hard time and a bunch of people were laughing. He agreed to meet, we set up a time, and I knew what I needed to do and say to make amends."

Andrew did meet him at which time his former victim pulled out a legal document which indicated that he and his brother were both changing their last name. He told Andrew that it was more than just he — lots of people had made fun of the name. But he did want Andrew to know how much pain he had inflicted on him. And the brothers were now causing more pain to their father and the family because that name had been theirs for many generations. He said the reason they were going to go through with it was that "I'll be damned if my kids are going to go through what my brother and I went through."

He didn't put all the blame on Andrew, but he did let Andrew know that his bullying at the party had left its mark. Andrew made amends based on his former victim's request and then called his brother. Andrew made a point to say that both brothers are brilliant guys. One works for Google in Chicago, and one is a mergers and acquisitions attorney in San Francisco.

"That day he really let me have it, he vented, but I was okay with that.

Strangely, the brother who lives here ended up asking me to list his house. It was an act of forgiveness. That's the thing about all of this; that's why I am so grateful for all of this. I'm really grateful for who I was at that age. I'm grateful for who I am getting to be this point. I wish, I certainly wish, there wasn't the collateral damage to the victims of the things I did. But, as a result of all of that, I've had these experiences where I'm able to see the connections between people that I don't normally get to see."

Andrew feels fortunate that he had all these experiences because now that he is a parent, he can apply much of what he has learned from them. He doesn't think that his parents ever really "got him." Having been a bully, having been a kid who hurt and made other kids suffer, then when you become a parent, a mature adult, you can understand the pain endured by the victim as well as the pain felt by the bully when all you want is for your kid to be happy.

PARENTING

Andrew's experience as a father has given him strong opinions about parenting today in our society. "Parenting is IT!!! To be a parent is this incredible gift, but it is also an obligation and responsibility. It is NOT to be taken likely. And I think our society does sometimes take parenting lightly. I'll use myself as an example — I love my kids, and I look at parenting as the best thing that's ever happened to me. Are there times when I want to shoo them away and I am not totally engaged with them? Sure! But that is not the deal. That's part of the problem from my perspective."

Andrew finds that his son Auggie is incredibly similar to himself. He's quirky, intelligent, and gifted, really an "old soul." He's not super athletic, although he could be if he wanted to be. He's artistic, he's curious, he's thoughtful, he's sensitive, and he's an amazing, amazing kid. For these reasons, mostly because he is quirky, Auggie will probably take a little more time, a little more effort, and a little more energy than the average second-grader. But what a thrill! What an opportunity! The same would be true of his brother Oscar, but from a different place. He's more athletic. It's fascinating to watch — Oscar pays more attention to what's happening in the outside world and where he measures up, whereas Auggie is somewhat oblivious at this point. Auggie just does his thing and Andrew observes as he watches Auggie, he gets ignored.

Andrew says, "So we try to allow him to be who he is, and we tell him that he should celebrate the fact that he is his own man. That his 'own man' should stand up for himself, and that it's okay not to be like everyone else.

Andrew shares a couple of stories to tell us how he feels about parenting and how his years as a bully have influenced his parenting skills.

"This is what I have done when Oscar or Auggie treat each other or others poorly. As I am driving home one day, my wife, Courtney, calls to tell me that Auggie punched Oscar in the nose, and there's blood all over. I can feel my own blood boil. Wanted to kill him for punching his brother. Fortunately, he was asleep by the time I got home. Courtney and I discussed it, and I asked, 'What are we going to do about this? How are we going to teach him that this is not all right, this is not okay? Tell you what I am going to do. I am going to wake him up at 6:30 tomorrow morning, and he is going to run up and down in the cul-de-sac, so he has a physical reminder of what he did. So that he understands.' That was my first idea.

"So, I woke up in the morning and went for a run. I asked myself, why would I have him do something physical when he has done something physical and mean to someone? Why would I not stop there and do something different? So, I woke Auggie at 6:30, and he and I went and got coffee. He knew exactly why I was getting him up. I told him he didn't get to have hot chocolate; this is not a reward time. He can have breakfast or water. So, we had this amazing conversation during which I explained to him about communicating versus using your fists. I explained to him what making amends means. I told him he was going to make an amends to his brother and make an amends to his mom.

"The actual cause for the punch was that he was not getting his way and his brother was talking to him and whatever. Unimportant. But what he got from our talk was fascinating. We came home, and Oscar was up, and Courtney was up, and I told Auggie, 'You need to make your amends.' So, he made his amends to Oscar. And he asked Oscar, 'What can I do?' and Oscar said, 'Please don't do that again.' Then Auggie recited, repeated what he and I had talked about. So, I knew he had absorbed our total conversation."

What Andrew and Courtney tell both boys now — in response to taunts or remarks from classmates — is this: People act that way because they are hurting inside, and it's the only way they know to tell you that they are hurting. We would like it if bullying didn't happen to them; we would like it if it never happens to any kid.

"I think about the victims, these kids who are killing themselves. Think about the level of hopelessness you would have to be at, at that young age, at an age when you should be totally carefree. Instead, because you don't fit in, you're the opposite of carefree."

Andrew also believes that as a parent you have to have the courage to tell another parent something — even if it is something very bad about what their child might have done, something that they might not know or be aware of. For example, there's this little boy in his kid's class, whose parents are friends of theirs. They're the sweetest, kindest people and their son is basically "a little blankety-blank," and they don't know it. He is somewhat like Andrew was at his age; similar to Eddie Haskell, real polite, but when his parents aren't around, he is being mean to the other kids. He's clearly got issues. There was a birthday party where this kid was breaking things and stuff, a real mess. A conversation took place among the parents who saw his behavior as to whether they should say something to the little boy's parents. Andrew said, "Yes, say something." He understood exactly because he was like that little boy. He knew how to manipulate the system, to push it to where if no one was looking he'd think he could get away with something, but if a parent asked, he would say he didn't do it.

Andrew's hope is that all kids get along and the minimum standard is absolute kindness to one another. As opposed to the minimum standard being — get along with the group you hang out with and don't worry about anybody else. Unfortunately, that is the way most of us believe. The point is that instead of three sets of parents having a conversation about whether to say something or not, there should be a procedure that has a parent saying, "Hey, if my kid is being a bully or not being one, I want to know." You, the parent, must always ask, "Why?"

CONCLUSION

Part of the catalyst for Andrew wanting to do this is that he can either hope that there will be an end to bullying or that he can take some kind of action to help bring about that end, to help banish bullying behavior. He believes that by sharing his story with kids, with his sons' classmates, and other classes, it might help them get a sense of what's going on in their lives. He thinks he has an obligation to share, to hone this story. And to try to make a difference for somebody else ... be it a bully or a victim, so the bully can stop bullying and the victim can find a way to connect with someone who can help him/her.

LESSONS LEARNED

There are many lessons to be learned from Andrew's story. He helps us understand the enormous pain experienced by some bullies. Once again, the behavior of these bullies should be considered a "call for help" by parents, teachers, workplace managers, and senior citizen caregivers. We know from long standing research that early intervention can make a significant difference in eliminating bullying behavior. Let us apply the lessons learned from Andrew in our response to the call for action to banish bullying behavior. We must provide appropriate intervention to help the bully, identify the root cause of his/her bullying behavior, be it insecurity, need for control, a traumatic experience such as parental divorce, being in pain, or being the victim of a bully. Once that is established, professional intervention should help the bully deal with the problems. This is the challenge that parents, educators, and workplace managers must address in order help banish bullying behavior.

Chapter Four

OVERVIEW OF WORKPLACE BULLYING

Stacy's stomach was in knots every Monday morning, the day of the weekly team meeting where she routinely had to endure ongoing mistreatment by her boss and team leader, Janine. At the nationally known charitable foundation where they both worked, Janine criticized Stacy when there was no reason for criticism, humiliated her, and withheld information and good assignments from her. Janine gave "the plum assignments" to the one man on the team and never advocated for Stacy. At times she bullied others as well, but Stacy was her prime target.

For twenty-one years Stacy worked for this highly respected foundation in California. When she returned to her hometown, Kansas City, she heard from a mutual friend that I was working on a book about workplace bullying. She offered to meet with me to discuss her experiences of being bullied by numerous colleagues during her tenure at the foundation. As we were concluding the interview, I asked Stacy why she had remained at that organization for so long.

"I believed in the organization's mission, and I loved my job," Stacy said. "The foundation was able to bring about significant change in the community and on a national level. It was very exciting to be able to develop programs and to see them implemented to bring about meaningful social and economic communal change."

I was aware of some of the outstanding contributions this foundation had made over the years, especially in the field of education. Thus, I found it ironic that such an organization would harbor bullies within its pristine walls.

The bullying started when Stacy had been there for three years; it was at that point her boss left and a new boss, Janine, took over. Stacy describes Janine as bright and attractive, in her late forties, a woman who "openly flirted with male colleagues." It was well known that Janine was married to a wealthy man and really did not need to work. She had no children and her coworkers believed that she worked because power and control factors fed her ego.

The behavior continued for five years, after which a new president took over and was appalled by the treatment of women at the foundation. He fired the perpetrators, including Janine, but a culture of bullying already had been established within the organization and continued throughout Stacy's entire tenure there.

Gary Namie, Ph.D., and Ruth Namie, Ph.D., founded the Workplace Bullying Institute (WBI) in response to just this kind of situation. In 1996 Ruth had been employed at a psychiatric clinic and had endured "a horrific woman supervisor." The Namies maintain that their principal purpose in creating the institute "is to help individuals caught in the web of lies spun by a bully at work to escape to safety as quickly as possible, to minimize harmful effects from exposure to undeserved stress." Within the structure of the WBI they conduct research, seminars, and a campaign for anti-bullying legislation. Their book *The Bully at Work: What You Can Do to Stop the Hurt and Reclaim Your Dignity on the Job* is considered one of the best in the field.

The WBI defines bullying as "repeated, health-harming mistreatment of one or more persons by one or more perpetrators. It is abusive conduct that is threatening, humiliating, or intimidating; or work interference — sabotage — which prevents work from getting done; or verbal abuse." The Namies draw a clear distinction between *harassment* and bullying. Harassment is illegal under state and federal laws. There is not yet any legislation that has been passed to make workplace bullying illegal; however, the Drs. Namie have been fighting this legislative battle state by state for many years.

Stacy is not the only person who has wanted to share her experiences of being bullied in the workplace; countless other individuals have been eager to tell me their stories as well. I've made a number of unexpected connections with total strangers who had heard through the grapevine that I was writing a book with a focus on workplace bullying. I discovered there are far more people than I would have imagined who have been bullied as adults in the workplace.

I've listened to dozens of targets' stories that encompass various types of workplace abuse. There are countless ways bullies carry out their hurtful actions in the workplace. The following are just a few examples.

UNWARRANTED OR INVALID CRITICISM

Janet went to work for the city of Boston directly out of college. From the beginning her boss criticized her, just as Stacy's boss had. Janet felt the criticism was trivial, unwarranted, and in some instances made no sense at all. In one occurrence her boss, Elaine, berated Janet for placing the coffee mug on the right side of Elaine's desk instead of the left. The morning following this criticism, she was rebuked for putting her boss's coffee mug on the left side instead of the right. Janet told me that she finally figured out that this type of bullying occurred after Elaine had had a fight with her boyfriend. It had nothing at all to do with Janet.

"I stuck it out for about a year, then decided to move on," Janet told me. "I wasn't about to let my work environment be dictated by my boss's love life."

I've heard stories similar to Janet's numerous times from people whose bosses brought their personal frustrations to work and took them out on their employees. No one should have to work in that type of environment, and a capable Human Resources department will intervene on behalf of the abused employee in a timely fashion.

BLAME WITHOUT FACTUAL JUSTIFICATION

Jack's coworker, Rick, repeatedly came to his desk and, in a loud voice, blamed him for one thing or another that he hadn't done. He'd blame Jack for interrupting him when he was on the phone, being late for team meetings, or spending too much time in the employees' lounge, when Jack had done nothing of the sort. This took place in a large open business office that had about a dozen desks in it. The coworker, a young upstart, had a shrill voice, and everyone around them could hear the accusations. Jack, a shy, retiring, middle-aged individual, found this humiliating and finally filed a report with Human Resources; unfortunately, the HR department where Jack worked was not up to speed on the seriousness of bullying in the workplace and did nothing. In no position to change jobs, Jack is still there toughing it out.

Among the people I interviewed about fifty percent found Human Resources to be very helpful. However, the other half have found themselves stuck in very stressful, and sometimes desperate, situations.

With the more recent recognition of the importance of a well-staffed, professional Human Resources department, management in many cases is making highly professional staffing a priority. Human Resources departments are also taking the initiative by conducting workshops and training for their employees to help prevent bullying and to help them recognize it when bullying does occur. I have been invited to conduct a number of these workshops and have received positive feedback from the participants, who found the information extremely helpful.

BEING TREATED DIFFERENTLY FROM
THE REST OF THE WORK GROUP

Sally had no idea why she was being treated differently from the rest of her work group. Her situation was similar to Stacy's. She was always the last person called on by her group leader during brainstorming sessions and was the last to receive her assignment, which was inevitably the least desirable one. Her colleagues tried to intervene on her behalf, but when they did this, the group leader ignored them.

This type of workplace bullying was recounted often during my interviews. Frequently those targeted in this way felt humiliated and experienced a total lack of support from the work group manager or leader.

BEING SWORN AT

At Abigail's entry-level job with a high-pressure political think tank in Washington, D.C., it was just a matter of course for people to use extremely foul language. But Abigail had grown up in a traditional Quaker community and was terribly uncomfortable when both her boss and her coworkers swore at her. By the time she changed jobs several years later, she was so accustomed to the swearing and screaming at her former job that she engaged in this very behavior herself without realizing it until her new boss pointed out that "we don't do that here."

Needless to say, she was mortified by her own behavior, but ultimately, she was thrilled with her new work environment. It made her very much aware of how one can get caught up in the culture of the workplace environment.

EXCLUSION OR SOCIAL ISOLATION

One of the most hurtful types of bullying at any age and in any setting is exclusion or social isolation. It can be just as painful for adults in the workplace as it is for children in grade school. Not welcoming a coworker at the lunchroom table or not inviting him or her to social gatherings after office hours, and then chattering about it the next day in front of that person — sometimes done with the intention to cause further hurt — are examples of workplace bullying that cuts deep. Many of the targets of this type of bullying who have shared their stories with me still feel the sting of exclusion and social isolation years later.

BEING A TARGET OF PRACTICAL JOKES

Tommy found himself being the target of repeated practical jokes that he did not find the least bit funny. The situation was so stressful that he spoke to his manager about it. She accused him of lacking a sense of humor and did nothing to change the situation. Finally, Tommy went to Human Resources and was again told that he lacked a sense of humor. He became so stressed that he had to take sick leave and ultimately was fired from his job.

Getting no assistance despite the series of steps that Tommy took is not an isolated situation. It is rather a common outcome following numerous types of bullying behavior. The target is bullied, goes to his or her supervisor and receives no support, goes to Human Resources and receives no support, has to take sick leave, and ultimately is fired. This pattern is reported again and again in newspaper articles and books about workplace bullying. As mentioned earlier, only about fifty percent of the people I interviewed found Human Resources to be "helpful," leaving the other fifty percent with inadequate support in a bad situation. For this reason, when considering taking a new job, it is so important to check out the Human Resources department to be certain you will get its support if necessary.

BEING SHOUTED AT OR BEING HUMILIATED

Abigail's and Jack's experiences of being shouted at and being humiliated are among the most common forms of workplace bullying. It is imperative for both employers and employees to be aware of this type of bullying behavior and address it head on.

If you are responsible for hiring new employees, be very specific and clear that your workplace has a zero-tolerance environment with respect to bullying behavior. During the interview process, an experienced interviewer can often note tendencies toward bullying behavior by observing the prospective employee's body language, as well as any overbearing effort to control the interview.

If you are on the other side of the table and are interviewing for a new position, be prepared to ask questions that will give you assurance that zero tolerance is actually enforced, and that bullying is not acceptable. This should be an important consideration in the decision of whether to take the job, if offered.

FACTORS THAT INCREASE THE RISK OF BULLYING BEHAVIOR

In a work setting, there are certain environmental factors that can increase the likelihood of bullying behavior. These risk factors include significant organizational shifts that create stress or insecurity among employees and supervisors alike, such as restructuring or technological changes. Even if those changes are beneficial, the upheaval can create anxiety or a feeling of lack of control, leading some individuals to act out. Preparing employees for significant organizational change can go a long way in preventing problems from arising.

Although bullying can happen in any environment and across all

**FIGURE 1:
CHECKLIST
FOR SUPERVISORS/MANAGERS
SELF-EVALUATION**

- ☐ Model/show respect
- ☐ Promote trust
- ☐ Promotes company values
- ☐ Team leader
- ☐ Open communication
- ☐ Agenda for weekly team meetings

- ☐ Good listener
- ☐ Clear expectations
- ☐ Assure job satisfaction
- ☐ Keep stress level low
- ☐ Promote job security

**FIGURE 2:
CHECKLIST
FOR TEAM MEMBER
SELF-EVALUATION**

- ❑ Feel respected
- ❑ Respectful to team members
- ❑ Feel valued
- ❑ Team player
- ❑ Confidence level

- ❑ Job comfort level
- ❑ Job security level
- ❑ Stress level
- ❑ Personal interactions
- ❑ Good communication

FIGURE 3:
CHECKLIST OF FACTORS THAT
MAY CAUSE BULLYING TO OCCUR

- ☐ Organization shifts
- ☐ Stress
- ☐ Insecurity
- ☐ Feeling of lack of control
- ☐ Lack of employee participation in decision making process
- ☐ Gender
- ☐ Apprentice/trainee status
- ☐ Rumors
- ☐ Flow of information
- ☐ Age

demographics, there are characteristics to be aware of among the individuals who make up a work team, especially when certain characteristics come into interaction. A person's age, gender, and apprentice or trainee status can be factors that affect personal interactions and sometimes lead to bullying behavior. For example, if a younger person is hired to become the supervisor of an employee of long standing, this can lead the older, established employee to feel insecure or not in control, which in turn can lead to bullying. Gender is another characteristic that often comes into play in workplace tensions. A woman I interviewed who was in a managerial role believed that a younger male employee who bullied her did so because the culture he came from didn't believe that women should be in a superior role to men.

Romantic relationships in the workplace sometimes play a significant role in workplace abuse, especially if and when a relationship sours. The injured partner in the relationship often spreads false rumors. Some individuals even end up stalking their former lover. For this reason, some organizations enforce a "no dating" policy.

Other important risk factors for workplace bullying are inadequate flow of information between organizational levels and lack of employee participation in the decision-making process.

All of these factors, when properly addressed, give employees a sense of security and control of their jobs — a strong antidote to bullying behavior. Among the numerous other factors that may add to the risk of workplace bullying are:

- Lack of policies about behavior;
- Heavy and intense workload;
- Staff shortages leading to heavy workloads;
- Interpersonal conflict;
- A supervisor's inability to set boundaries and limits; and
- Lack of authority at various levels of management.

There are many who advocate for the use of checklists. In his book *The Checklist Manifesto: How to Get Things Right,* Atul Gawande makes a compelling case for the simple checklist to bring about improvement in our daily lives, given the rapidly growing complexity of our world. This would also hold true for our workplace lives, and Gawande demonstrates the use of checklists in his own workplace. Creating a checklist of the factors discussed here could go a long way in preventing bullying behavior from occurring. With such a checklist, management could identify and remedy risk factors before bullying even starts. In the event of a bullying situation, a checklist could be used as part of the solution, allowing management to identify what underlying causes may have contributed to the problem. With that information the behavior can be addressed and eliminated. We should note that the same checklists could be given to employees, as well, to provide them with a feeling of being in the loop and having a sense of control.

WORKPLACE BULLYING STATISTICS

How widespread is bullying in the workplace? A total of 65.6 million people have been affected by workplace bullying, based on surveys conducted by the WBI. It is important to keep in mind that each of these situations represents enormous pain for each and every person involved. That's deep individual pain multiplied by 65.6 million. This, the first national scientific survey of workplace bullying, was conducted by the WBI and Zogby International. The poll surveyed 7,740 adult Americans in the summer of 2007. Based on this poll, we know that one in three employees experienced bullying at some point in their working lives. Put another way this means that, in a company of one hundred employees, more than thirty of these workers are bullied at some point during their careers. If we count *everyone* who is harmed by bullying, including witnesses, then nearly half of all Americans have been affected by workplace bullying (as a target, a victim, or a witness). Follow-up reports conducted during 2010 and one in January 2014 by Zogby Analytics of one thousand adults found the results to be very similar in many areas to the earlier survey. However, the number of employees experiencing abusive conduct at work has declined to twenty-seven percent from thirty-three percent. At least the movement is in the right direction! Clearly the fact that the "silent epidemic" has been given a voice and is being addressed is having a positive effect on the workplace environment.

Based on the 2014 survey 40.1 percent of those interviewed said bosses were the primary perpetrators of bullying and abusive conduct in

U.S. workplaces. Fifty-six percent responded that the bully held a higher rank than the victim; thirty-three percent indicated that the abuse came from peers; and eleven percent said the perpetrators were subordinates. Sixty-nine percent of those surveyed reported that the bullies were men, and thirty-one percent reported that they were women. In addition, among those surveyed who had actually experienced or witnessed bullying, Sixty percent reported that the targets were women, and forty percent said they were men.

At the time the Drs. Namie received the results of the initial survey they called workplace bullying a "silent epidemic." Although they have played an important role in removing the silent aspect of bullying in the workplace, the statistics are an important reminder of the epidemic proportions of workplace abuse.

A LOOK AT THE WIDER CONTEXT

Workplace bullying often starts at home. An estimated fifty percent of school bullies have been bullied at home by one or both of their parents and/or one or more siblings. Unless there is early intervention, these same school bullies will grow up to become workplace bullies. There is also a good chance that many of the parents who bully their children at home also bully in the workplace.

Bullying has long been considered a learned behavior, one that is often discovered at a very young age. The bully realizes early on that his or her size, strength, or verbal talent could be a highly effective tool with respect to social behavior. Many of the targets I interviewed maintained that the bullies they observed had a need for control, a desire to exert power, or seemed very competitive.

Dr. Moira Mulhern, co-founder and executive director of Turning Point: The Center for Hope and Healing, has found that bullies often react aggressively in response to perceived provocation, insults, or slights. It is not clear whether the act of bullying gives them pleasure or whether it's simply the way they've learned to get what they want.

"Bullies come in many forms and sizes," Dr. Mulhern explained. "Universally they have deep-seated psychological problems — inferiority, inadequacy, and serious problems relating to others."

Bullies with more serious problems are considered to be psychopathic. These individuals are callous, vindictive, and controlling, with little or no empathy or concern for the rights and feelings of their victims, no matter what the context. They do not feel remorse or guilt. They lack insight into their own behavior and are either unwilling or unable to moderate it. Their behavior is similar to the behavior of manipulators in the workplace. It is imperative for management and supervisors to recognize these psychopathic behaviors and to make professional referrals for the individuals to get the appropriate help to address their serious problems.

Workplace bullies often get away with their behavior because managers prefer to avoid messy, interpersonal conflict and shrug off episodes as "personal matters," rather than seeing them as work-related problems. In some cases, the employees who are bullies can be very competent at their jobs, and their employers do not want to lose their valuable skills. Workplace bullies often operate within the established rules and policies of their organizations, therefore leaving no recourse on the part of the victims. Abigail's story is a perfect example of this type of workplace bullying. She, with her Quaker background, found herself in a workplace environment where shouting and swearing at one another were the organization's normal behavior. No one within the structure of the organization considered this to be bullying behavior. It was "business as usual" for this Washington, D.C., workplace, but the new employee, Abigail, felt like she was being bullied until it became a new norm for her.

Bullies view their workplace targets, like their targets in general, as weak and vulnerable. By contrast, some targets are more competent professionally than their aggressors and refuse to be intimidated. This can make the bully feel insecure, a very common characteristic leading to bullying behavior. Workplace bullies often target colleagues whose success they envy, jealousy being a major factor in their behavior.

HEALTH ISSUES RELATED TO BULLYING
IN THE WORKPLACE

A number of health issues are directly related to workplace bullying. The stress this abusive behavior puts on targets and victims can become a major factor in their psychological and physical health. Several people I interviewed had been told by their physicians that they didn't need more medications; they were advised instead to change their jobs to reduce the stress they were experiencing by being bullied in their place of employment. Fortunately, with the upturn of the economy some of them were successful in finding new jobs in a better work environment.

PSYCHOLOGICAL FACTORS

The psychological impact of bullying is well documented. Targets of workplace bullying report serious bouts of anxiety as a result of their experiences, as well as sleeplessness, obsession over the situation, clinical depression, and self-destructive behavior, such as increased consumption of drugs, alcohol, and food. They report having thoughts of committing violence against others, as well as suicidal impulses.

The most predominant health factor reported by victims of bullying in the workplace is stress, a biological process triggered by a source known as the *stressor*. Because the bully chooses the individual to be targeted and controls the onset and termination of attacks, as well the nature and severity of psychological violence inflicted, the bully is considered the stressor — the source of the target's stress. The response of the body and the mind to stressors determines the extent of the damage. Jack, mentioned earlier in this chapter, is an example of someone who has not omitted the stressor from his life by leaving his job. He is still toughing it out, but at a heavy price. He experiences regular bouts of anxiety and depression.

BIOLOGICAL FACTORS

The biological health impact of stress is enormous. Almost fifty percent of the targets of workplace bullying have been diagnosed with panic attacks, heart palpitations, or an elevated heart rate. Forty-five percent suffer from exhaustion, and almost the same number experience fatigue syndrome or connective tissue problems, joint pain, and weight swings. Headaches — from mild to migraine — are also a common health factor. Additional biological symptoms include Irritable Bowel Syndrome (IBS), chest pains, stress-related skin changes — such as shingles, eczema, and similar ailments — and hypertension.

Three decades after leaving the high-pressure political think tank where everyone yelled and swore, Abigail still lives in Washington, D.C., with her family. In spite of the fact that she works now in a positive environment she still suffers from just about every stress-related health issue listed here. I have observed her weight swings, headaches, IBS, and skin-related issues.

When the stress caused by bullying is sudden, severe, prolonged, and/or repetitive or when the attack humiliates the victim or destroys the victim's community and support system, the person being bullied can develop Post-Traumatic Stress Disorder (PTSD).

The following are symptoms of PTSD:
- Feeling edgy, easily startled, constantly on guard
- Experiencing recurrent unpleasant memories, nightmares, or flashbacks
- Needing to avoid traumatizing feelings, thoughts, locations, or situations
- Insomnia

Coworkers who witness bullying behavior — even if they are not targeted themselves — often experience negative effects, as well. They can undergo stress, fear, and emotional exhaustion just from having witnessed bullying. Witnesses often choose to leave a job at a workplace where bullying occurs, given the opportunity to do so.

THE EPIGENETIC FACTOR

Epigenetics is the study of how genetic traits can change and be changed within a single generation and can even be passed down to a new generation. It is the study of cellular and physiological trait variations that are **not** caused by the DNA sequence, but instead by external or environmental factors that turn genes on and off and affect how cells read genes. This is a new area of research pioneered within the last several decades by Michael Meaney, Ph.D., and Moshe Szyf, Ph.D., at McGill University and Louise Arseneault, Ph.D., at King's College in London, along with their research groups.

Sharon Moalem, M.D., reports the results of their work in layman's terms in his book *Inheritance: How Our Genes Change Our Lives and Our Lives Change Our Genes*. These two groups of researchers studied sets of monozygotic (identical) twins at the age of five. In addition to having identical DNA, each twin in the study had not been bullied. The twins had been revisited at the age of twelve, and only one in each pair had been bullied. They found "a striking epigenetic difference that was not there when the children were five years old." Significant changes were evident only in the twin who had been bullied (in response to the ongoing stress of being bullied).

"This means in no uncertain genetic terms that bullying isn't just risky in terms of self-harming tendencies for youth and adolescents," Dr. Moalem writes. "It actually changes how our genes work and how they change our lives, and likely what we are passing on to future generations. The reason these findings are significant is that these epigenetic changes are thought to be able to persist throughout our lives. This means that even if you can't remember the details of being bullied, your genes certainly do."

He warns that these epigenetic changes can cause serious long-term psychiatric conditions, such as depression and alcoholism, and that they are likely heritable from one generation to the next. Although these findings are based on childhood bullying, it has obvious impact on adult life and workplace bullying, as well.

In another study Isabelle Ouellet-Morin, Ph.D., affiliated with King's College, London, and the University of Montreal, and her research team looked at thirty pairs of identical twins born between 1994 and 1995, collecting their data through the British Environmental Risk (E-Risk) Twin Study. The researchers concentrated on these thirty pairs of 2,232 British children from 1,116 families in the overall study. The twins came from all walks of life in England and Wales. They specifically "tested whether bullying victimization, a repeated adverse experience in childhood, influences cortisol responses to a psychosocial stress test (PST) using a discordant monozygotic (MZ) families with twins."

The team of researchers reported that they found "blunted cortisol responses to stress in bullied twins in comparison with their non-bullied co-twins." They concluded that the bullied victims were inhibited from having a normal reaction to being abused. Because the subjects were identical twins, the difference could not be attributed to genetic differences, nor could it be caused by environmental factors since they were raised in the same homes. "The difference," the researchers concluded, "came from changes in gene expression through epigenetics that left the victims less responsive to stress."

As the lead author of the study Dr. Ouellet-Morin said, "If we accept the idea suggested by this study, that social environment can change DNA manipulation that is important for stress reactivity and mood regulation, then if we change that environment, if we make sure the victims are not victimized anymore, or if we give them the proper resources to cope better with the situation and get on with their lives, then we have the possibility of reversing what we are observing right now."

These studies are subsets of the research that investigates how genetic and environmental factors, nature and nurture, shape children's disruptive behavior. It is an ongoing study looking at the twins at ages five, seven, twelve, and most recently eighteen.

Stress is an integral and pervasive factor in workplace bullying, as we have seen throughout the discussion in this chapter. Fortunately, recognition of that fact and research in that area bode well for the future.

I am still amazed at the number of people who sought me out to share their personal experiences with workplace bullying; to my mind, this indicates how far reaching this epidemic is and the tremendous need to address it. The passion with which some have responded to the subject was at times surprising. For a brief period, I had decided to give up on the idea of writing this book, and I shared that information during a university guest lecture. In response, one individual, a doctoral student, jumped out of her seat and practically yelled, "You MUST write the book!" We met for coffee, and she obviously made a very compelling case for me to complete my work on this book! In a management position at a very large insurance company, she had had horrific bullying experiences early in her career. Her dissertation topic was "Civility in the Business World."

The targets and victims you met in this chapter represent a small cross-section of the types of bullying encountered in the workplace at large. In the next chapter you will meet individuals in the workplaces of medicine, law, and academia, in particular — all well-known bullying workplace environments. Highly accomplished, busy people in all three professions spent many hours giving me in-depth interviews. They all shared a passionate belief that workplace bullying is an extremely serious problem that must be addressed. By telling their stories, they have joined me in responding to the urgent call for action.

Chapter Five

BULLYING IN SPECIFIC WORKPLACE VENUES

Individuals in each of the specific workplace venues studied for this chapter maintained that **their** respective workplaces suffered from **the** most serious workplace bullying. However, it is interesting to note how many similar factors influenced the environment of all the venues studied.

IN THE FIELD OF MEDICINE

For several months I had been suffering from an idiopathic medical condition. A complete medical workup at the Kansas University Medical Center followed by another at the Mayo Clinic found no cause for my ailment. A friend who is a physician in Boston referred me to one of his colleagues, Dr. Valerie Watson. She is in her mid-forties and has established an excellent reputation as an outstanding diagnostician.

It became evident immediately during the "get to know you" portion of my first appointment with Dr. Watson she was interested in "the whole person." When she heard that I was writing my third book on bullying, this one focusing on workplace bullying, she said, "you know that there is an enormous amount of workplace bullying in the field of medicine, and women have been the prime targets for over 150 years. I had my first bullying experience during my third year of medical school. I was totally humiliated and have shared this story with very few people."

She explained, "When I was eleven years old, I was the tallest girl in my class and my father teased me that if I didn't stop growing I would never find a husband! I didn't grow another inch and at five-feet-two inches had a tendency to be a bit pudgy, never fat, but a bit on the heavy side."

Today, Dr. Watson is a beautiful woman with a ready smile, a twinkle in her blue eyes, a chic hairstyle, and a fashionable outfit under her white coat. She is wife and mother of four children.

She continued, "It is generally accepted that bullying of medical students takes place in their third year, and that was also true in my case. One day during medical rounds, Dr. Jones, a physician on staff, turned to me and out of nowhere said, 'Watson if you lost a little weight and stopped snacking so much you would have a better sex life.' I know I turned bright red and was totally humiliated.

"Dr. Jones had the reputation for saying the most absurd, outrageous things to medical students, colleagues and even patients. He got away with it because of his excellent reputation as a physician."

Dr. Watson confessed that she told this story to very few people, but hearing the term "workplace bullying" opened the floodgates. Apparently, Dr. Watson's experience is much more common than the average layman would expect.

Dr. Pauline Chen reported on "The Bullying Culture of Medical School" in a *New York Times* Internet post in August of 2012. Early studies indicate that as many as eighty-five percent of medical students were bullied the year they started working one-on-one or in small teams with senior physicians and residents in the hospital. The abuse included name-calling, threats of a poor grade or a ruined career, being hit, shoved, humiliated, and even having a medical instrument thrown at them.

Having identified the bullying culture of medical schools, medical educators throughout the country thought that this abusive behavior could be eliminated or at least brought under control if all medical schools acknowledged the behavior, created institutional anti-harassment policies, grievance committees, educational training, and counseling programs to break the abuse cycle.

In 1995, the David Geffan School of Medicine at the University of California Los Angeles initiated a comprehensive program including all the elements described above. At the end of their third year of medical school students were given a five-question survey to ascertain the amount of bullying they experienced during this crucial year. At the end of thirteen years the survey results indicated that more than half of all the medical students still reported being intimidated physically or verbally. The National Medical Education survey reported approximately the same results.

Dr. Moira Mulhern is an expert on resilience and frequently deals with bullying in the field of medicine. As mentioned earlier she is the co-founder and executive director of Turning Point: The Center for Hope and Healing, a support center provides a comprehensive social and emotional support system and education to individuals, their families and friends, living with cancer and other serious or chronic illnesses. She is very involved in the field of medicine.

She is often called on to make presentations in hospitals and other medical institutions. Dr. Mulhern gives an initial general talk on bullying and asks for feedback on specific problems. She then returns to meet with smaller groups to address issues such as lack of communication, lack of emotional intelligence, and a need for change in perfectionistic thought patterns specific to health care environments.

Dr. Mulhern has found that in health care institutions where there appears to be a theme of perfectionistic, critical thought processes it is not uncommon to hear accounts of surgeons scolding nurses or other doctors, demeaning students such as Dr. Watson experienced, as well as residents in groups or alone. Perfectionists who become aware that their behavior is bullying will try to temper their critical demeanor and work to change their tone. However, most often they will need some coaching on how to let go of their critical thought patterns. Perfectionists are reluctant to let go of the behavior because they are attached to their high standards.

When they realize they can keep their high standards and let go of the critical piece they're more likely to listen to coaches and attempt change. Perfectionists do not want to be seen as a bully — they just want others "to do it right."

Dr. Mulhern has found that bullies in medicine who are not perfectionists often are immature and emotionally low functioning. Although harder to change this, too, can be remediated with the right coaching and a lot of practice.

"When talking to a group where I know there are bullies, I have seen the light go on with some people when I tell them that a group is low-functioning and immature. In other words, they come to the realization of how poorly their behavior reflects on them as individuals," Dr. Mulhern told me.

There seems to be a difference between a closed-hospital system (where doctors are employees of the hospital) and an open-hospital system (where doctors are on time-limited contracts). When doctors are employees of the hospital, the hospital has more control over their behavior whereas in an open system the doctors have privileges, such as the right to admit patients and the use of the hospital facilities, and can take their business to another hospital. In the latter situation there is less control over a doctor's abusive bullying behavior. More bullying is also reported when the hospital administration does not enforce a "people first" culture. In an open system, if the administration looks the other way in order to retain a highly skilled physician or nurse, it is perpetuating a culture of bullying.

"I don't think enough attention is given to analysis of the whole system. Take a look at the leader at the top and the leaders of different work groups all the way down: Strong leaders will foster a higher functioning, supportive, and happier environment," Dr. Mulhern said.

THE FIELD OF LAW

Ann, who is now a partner in a prestigious law firm in St. Louis, Missouri told me that the only bully-free environment she worked in during her career was when she clerked for a federal judge. She said the chief justice insisted that everyone in her courtroom was to be treated with respect, from the janitor to the clerks to the most eminent lawyer. The emphasis in the courtroom was on "civility," and "it was wonderful."

Her experience in a 900-person law firm with offices nationally and internationally has been quite different. In spite of the fact that the lawyers go through extensive training as first-year associates on "how to treat your secretary and colleagues, as well as on social relationships," there is a tremendous amount of bullying behavior that goes on among young associates as well as with partners. She gave me the example of one very senior partner whose behavior was so "awful" he was sent to anger management classes several times by his partners. Even though his behavior persists, the partner is still retained by the firm because he is such an outstanding attorney.

I conducted extensive interviews with senior partners, junior associates and summer interns in large (900 attorneys), medium (400 attorneys), and boutique-small law firms, and there is general agreement that bullying behavior is rampant in the field of law. Women and young lawyers are the most frequent targets of the bullies.

Some attorneys suggested that the legal profession attracts "bright, overachieving" individuals who use the "power" inherent in the field to feed their bullying behavior. Others maintained that the field also attracts very competitive individuals, which can lead to all sorts of abusive behavior. One attorney gave the example of a young associate handing off work to another young associate in order "to make him look bad."

Just as in other workplace environments, bullying in law offices manifests itself through cursing, name-calling, and sometimes even physical intimidation. Because of the hierarchical nature of the practice of law, there is an unequal power structure that leads bullies to demean the legal position of their targets. Young associates are assigned such menial tasks that they often wonder why they chose to enter the field of law. The long hours and pressure to "bill hours" also feed the power of bullies from above. One lawyer described it as using the tone of "wait until your father gets home." The threat of intervention from above, senior partners, creates an environment similar to what a child experiences when his punishment is not administered until his father comes home.

All the lawyers I interviewed talked about how much bullying behavior is directed at young associates. "You're a young punk and don't know what you're talking about" is repeated time again and again in law offices as well as in the courtrooms. A variation on that theme is: "Only a young, inexperienced attorney would make such an accusation."

The three most frequently used terms in bullying in the law as reported in the literature, as well as in my interviews are — "inept, ignorant, and inexperienced." This type of bullying has been reported in the literature as leading to loss of confidence in the ability and the work among young lawyers.

A tremendous amount of bullying takes place right in the courtroom. Some lawyers I spoke with expressed the opinion that judges could and should do a better job of intervening in those instances. Some lawyers seem to feel that, in order to "advocate and protect their clients," they need to ridicule and reduce the opposing clients to tears. One lawyer described an experience in court in which the opposing attorney simply sat there and stared at him for hours on end.

Another attorney told me that bullies in the profession of law "justify their behavior because they perceive themselves as powerful, which is advantageous for their clients. They enjoy the reputation this gives them, and they believe this is beneficial for success."

ACADEMIA

Melanie and Steve were high school sweethearts. They met when Steve was a senior and Melanie was a sophomore and dated for five years before they were married. Steve had just started medical school and Melanie was a junior in college at the time of their marriage. When she graduated, she worked to put Steve through medical school "with some help from both sets of parents."

Steve was invited to join a prestigious medical practice when he completed his medical training. Melanie no longer had to be the breadwinner of their family and was able to enter a doctoral program in psychology at the University. She and Steve enjoyed sharing the parenting of their children, and Steve was very supportive of Melanie's work.

Toward the end of her doctoral program one of her fellow doctoral candidates said to Melanie, "We were wondering whether you and Professor Smith were having an affair." Melanie told me that she was left speechless by the inquiry on two counts. First, that she had been the topic of department gossip, and second, that they would even think she would have an affair, code word for "sleep with" Dr. Smith. Both she and her professor were happily married. All their meetings were in Dr. Smith's office, never off campus. "When I vehemently denied it my colleague said, 'We didn't think so, but we were just curious!'"

There were seven professors in the department, all married, and four were having affairs with students. Two professors actually divorced their wives and married their doctoral advisees. The other two just seemed to have worked out some sort of arrangement with their wives and their doctoral students/candidates, Melanie told me. To put it crassly, the professors bully their students to sleep with them. They threaten them with failing grades and possibly failing the program. Students are bullied to do an excessive amount of departmental work such as grading papers or research without getting credit for it.

As I conducted my interviews on bullying in academia, I found that Melanie's story was not that unusual. One doctoral candidate, Anna, a single mom, told me that she had had an affair with a member of her doctoral committee, and when she wanted to break it off she had to have a restraining order placed on the professor. Anna shared her story with her female advisor, who said, "Get over it. We all slept with Professor So-and-So when we went through our doctoral programs."

Bob told me that during his doctoral program he lived in university married students' housing with his wife and young daughter. The son of another doctoral student living in the same housing bullied Bob's daughter to such an extent he had to report it to the university administration. The bully's father made life so unpleasant for Bob that he had to leave the University and never did complete his doctoral program. One of the witnesses to this saga told me that it was really a tragedy, that Bob was outstanding in his field and should have had a bright future. No one knows what happened to Bob and his family after they left the university.

The pervasive nature of bullying in academia is reported in numerous studies conducted in the United States and abroad since 1990. They underscore the fact that childhood bullying continues into adulthood and the professional life of those working in academia at all levels. Individuals who moved to higher education from K-12 have been heard to comment, "These are the same bullies we used to talk about in the teachers' lounge."

The nature of bullying in the academic environment is very similar to workplace bullying in most environments. It can be found at all levels of academia as reported by Leah P. Hollis, ED.E., in her book *Bully in the Ivory Tower*. She compared the amount of bullying directed at targets starting with college and university entry-level jobs, assistant director, director, non-tenured faculty, tenured faculty, assistant/associate dean, dean, assistant/associate vice-president, vice-president provost, president and other. Not surprisingly, she found the largest amount of targeting was at people in the entry-level jobs (28.8 percent) and the least amount of targeting was by the president.

For the purpose of her study she coined the term *vicarious* bullying. Dr. Hollis maintains, "Often a leader or manager empowers a secretary, assistant or fellow staffer to wield his or her power. While this manager is not directly showing aggression, his/her power is extended through an appointed subordinate." Dr. Hollis gives the example of a college president sending out his executive secretary to exert bullying behavior at a staffer by humiliating her at a staff meeting for not getting a report in on time.

Dr. Hollis also addressed the intersection of bullying and harassment, using the term *bullrassment*. This refers to bullying/harassment of people who don't have the protected status of Title VII. Target of bullying is not included as protected status under Title VII. For many years there has been ongoing movement to get protected status for targets and victims of workplace bullying with no success yet at the time of this writing.

A leadership model for a healthy workplace in academia has been developed by Dr. Hollis. Her model also is based on the importance of executive leadership, leadership based on building trust and transparency from top to bottom. She stresses that access and visibility are both very important for those who are in leadership positions. Two additional components of her leadership model are accountability and civility. It will be interesting to see if the results of her study are implemented and have a significant positive impact on workplace bullying in academia.

IN THE LOCKER ROOM

For months the Miami Dolphins' "Classic Case of Bullying" not only dominated the sports pages across the country but the front pages as well. Richie Incognito, John Jerry, and Mike Pouncey became household names as the tormentor of Jonathan Martin.

Ted Wells, a defense lawyer, was hired by the NFL to investigate the allegations of bullying within the Dolphins' organization. The 144-page report portrayed the life of the players "in extraordinary and unseemly detail." His report was based on emails, text messages, and more than one hundred interviews with Miami personnel, including players, coaches, management, and support staff. It was reported members of the staff were also victims of the same bullies. For example, an assistant coach who was born in Japan was "jokingly threatened" on the anniversary off Pearl Harbor in retaliation for the Pearl Harbor attack. The unnamed assistant coach confided in Martin, who in turn shared numerous episodes with interviewers for the report.

An example of classic middle school bullying behavior was reported: "When Martin was waiting in the cafeteria line for dinner, Incognito called him a derogatory term and told him not to join them for dinner. When Martin tried to sit down at their table, they left, and he (Martin) flung his tray on the floor and left the building. Martin checked himself into a hospital to receive psychiatric services." The report is filled with similar episodes and ugly text messages.

The report concluded that the harassment of Jonathan Martin resembled "a classic case of bullying, where persons who are in a position of power harass the less powerful." Attorney Wells concluded, "We encourage the creation of new workplace conduct rules and guidelines that will ensure that players respect each other as professionals and people."

Chapter Six

LEADERSHIP, LEADERSHIP, LEADERSHIP . . .

The difference between a healthy workplace environment and a toxic one starts with the leadership at the top and continues with the leadership at all levels of the organization. Whether it is the lack of leadership at Stacy's California Foundation or JeT'aime's strong leadership at Sugar and Spice Salon and Spa in St. Thomas, U.S. Virgin Islands, it all comes down to leadership.

Sugar and Spice Salon and Spa is tucked away in a corner of Yacht Haven Grande on the island. My husband, Neil, and I went there for haircuts and foot care, and I left there with a truly inspiring lesson in leadership. I knew as soon as we walked through the door that this was a very special place. Neil and I were greeted warmly by Gina and Jocelyn as if we were guests in their home.

We started off seated side-by-side for our foot care; when Jocelyn had finished with Neil she led him to the barber chair for his haircut, and Gina promptly set to scrubbing Jocelyn's foot tub. Moments later Jocelyn quietly thanked Gina. Stylists swept up after each other's haircuts and offered fellow stylists' clients liquid refreshments. This type of teamwork could be observed among all the stylists in the salon. This was teamwork at its best.

While JeT'aime, the owner of the salon and spa, was cutting my hair I told her about the research and interviews I was conducting on workplace bullying and asked her if she would tell me how she had created such a special work environment. She was most forthcoming and articulate in her response.

Before she hires anyone new, she conducts an in-depth interview with the prospective employee. In addition to assessing experience and skills, she stresses the importance of teamwork and a "no gossip," rule that are both strictly enforced. New employees are given extensive on-the-job training, so they are comfortable and confident in their work. She also stresses the importance of good communication, and to ensure this she holds weekly meetings with her entire staff of ten stylists. She also told me that she is good at reading body language, and "if an employee walks through the door in the morning and I can tell by his/her body language there seems to be a problem, we have a talk before we begin our day's work."

I asked JeT'aime whether she ever had to fire anyone, and she replied in the affirmative. "I think I give employees too much time to make the grade, but usually the problem is their inability to work as part of the team. In spite of all the time we spend on the importance of teamwork during the interview, some employees just 'don't seem to get it' on the job." She said this is the main reason she has to let a stylist go — for inability to be part of their team — rarely for a lack of professional skill, and "I tell them so!"

Before she was able to pay rent for a salon, JeT'aime began as a "nomadic hair stylist" with a team of three, traveling to people's homes, and now she owns an award-winning salon and spa with her staff of ten. Being a "nomadic hair stylist" lent itself well to doing the hair for bridal parties, and as such she established herself as the "go-to" person for wedding parties on the island. Hers is truly a wonderful success story, and her business has been recognized as "The Best Salon on the Virgin Islands" every year since 2011. JeT'aime herself has been recognized as "The Best Hair Stylist on the Virgin Islands" and received the Entrepreneur of the Year Award in 2010.

JeT'aime's successful small business reflects much of the research literature available in all fields of endeavor. Her leadership, emphasis on teamwork, her interview process, on-the-job training program, and support for her staff are all important components of a healthy workplace. She made it very clear to me that her employees are her most important resource.

The healthy workplace environment starts with strong leadership at the top; equally important is clear leadership at all levels of management — by managers, supervisors, and team leaders, depending on the organizational structure. Leaders must demonstrate integrity and earn a strong measure of trust from their employees.

The Kansas City Business Journal selects the metropolitan area's "Best Places to Work" each year based on a survey of the employees. They rate their workplaces in regard to team managers' effectiveness, job security, work management, and whether employees feel valued — in addition to numerous other healthy workplace environment factors. Any company in the metropolitan area with ten or more full-time employees is eligible to become a "Best Place to Work" based on the survey, which is administered by an independent agency.

Parris Communications, Inc., has been named one of the "Best Places to Work" in the Kansas City area each year since 2007. They have also taken first place in the small business category. Founded in 1988 by Roshann Parris, the firm has established a reputation for corporate communications campaigns and crisis management nationwide.

"Being a Best Place to Work not only feels good to those who live in it, but it is also good for business," Parris said. "One of the things that I think may be the most undervalued and also the most true about creating a Best Place to Work is that it's simply great for business. A happy team begets great work that begets clients who get unsurpassed attention and client service second to none. So, being a Best Place to Work not only feels good to those who live in it, but it is also good for business," Parris repeated.

Katja Edelman, who was a summer intern at Parris Communications, Inc., believes that the open atmosphere is probably a major part of why people like working there so much. "There are regular meetings when everyone checks in with their projects; support is offered openly and non-judgmentally. Everyone seems to enjoy his or her work; that probably plays a major role in overall happiness."

At these meetings if someone is struggling with an aspect of his or her project everyone jumps in to help. Whether it is the public relations team, marketing or communications they all help and support the entire staff's work. This is also true of the professionals working in the areas of strategic corporate communications, media relations, and crisis communication. There is enough sharing of information about their respective team projects at the regular meetings to enable the whole staff to brainstorm and support one another's individual teams project.

I've watched Parris Communications grow from Roshann and one assistant to a staff of ten high-powered extraordinarily talented individuals, each with his or her own portfolio. The staff's professionalism as well as their personal warmth have always impressed me. During our interview Roshann urged me to convey the importance of "the team."

The chief operating officer, Laurie Roberts, makes it possible for Roshann Parris also to use her leadership ability to serve as a lead advance person on the Presidential Advance Team accompanying President Bill Clinton and Mrs. Clinton to over fifty countries on their travels worldwide. This is clearly a healthy workplace operating with outstanding leadership and teamwork.

The World's Best Multinational Workplace List makes the importance of a healthy workplace environment very clear. It examines workplace culture, levels of employee trust, camaraderie, and pride, all of which are factors in determining employee engagement and business success. There are 6,200 companies that are reviewed representing 11.9 million employees. Google was the top company on the Twenty-five Absolute Best Workplaces in the World list, reported in the October 2014 edition of *Entrepreneur*. Microsoft, Marriott, and e-Bay were also included on the top twenty-five list.

In an ideal workplace, the values of the organization, whether in the field of medicine, law, academia, sports, or business, should be an integral part of all areas of the culture and environment. They should be modeled by the top leaders of the business all through the ranks and during the interview with the prospective employee. From the moment a prospective employee sits down to an interview, the company's core values should be in play. If open communication and teamwork are central, those values should be discussed or even exhibited.

The interview process should work two ways, enabling both employer and prospective employee to ascertain whether the hire would be a good fit. It is very important for the employer to convey the value placed on teamwork, respect, job satisfaction and good communication on all levels. Job expectations are an important topic to cover at the interview. In many larger companies more than one person interviews prospective employees. This is a good opportunity for the interviewee to evaluate whether the job expectations are in sync. Several of the people I interviewed indicated that job expectations were very different from what were discussed during the interview, in some cases leading to serious misfits and workplace problems.

An experienced interviewer is often able to detect behaviors during the interview process that might indicate a tendency toward bullying, such as controlling behavior or power plays. Equally, an astute prospective employee can pick up on the leadership dynamic of the interviewer that could be a reflection of the leadership within the company as a whole. The interview also gives the candidate the opportunity to ask questions that will give him/her a feel for the type of work environment within the organization. A key question should be what the rate of turnover is in relation to the rate of retention. If the turnover rate is high, that should serve as a red flag that there might be a bully factor at work.

Job interviews are very serious business. However, they also have their lighter moments as illustrated by this story Maria shared with me. As a young law school graduate, she interviewed for a job with a prestigious Washington, D.C., law firm. She had good credentials: an undergraduate degree from Yale and a law degree from Michigan Law School. The interview seemed to go well, and at the end the interviewer asked if Maria had any additional questions. Without thinking she asked how much vacation time they offered. As soon as the words were out of her mouth she thought, "OMG, I don't even have the job, and they are going to think all I care about is vacation!"

Her credentials and personality carried the day she did get the job but discovered that the 900-person law firm was not a good fit and left for a small law firm after two years.

As was illustrated in the story of JeT'aime's Salon, the on-the-job training process is key for providing a new employee with the confidence to do his or her job well. It also creates a certain comfort level in the new work environment. In addition to focusing on skill building, training should emphasize respectful behavior toward all colleagues and fellow employees of the organizational hierarchy, from the janitor to the secretary to the company president.

Communication skills, including the ability to be a good listener, are an important component of the training process. Stress management should also be taught to enable employees to cope better if and when periods of stress occur. Even in the best of circumstances, most jobs do have periods of stress.

Conveying to all of the employees that the organization's leadership understands that **they** are the company's most valued resource goes a long way in creating a healthy work environment and culture. Including employees in the decision-making process gives them a sense of belonging and ownership in the success of the organization.

Even businesses and organizations that have been healthy workplaces for generations suddenly find themselves with a bully in their midst. The cardiology practice of Thompson and Thompson recently found itself in that situation. Dr. Byron Thompson opened his medical practice in the 1930s, during the depression. He, like so many of his colleagues in that generation, often recalled being paid whatever their patients could afford — including eggs, chickens, or fresh produce.

His son, Allan, joined his father's medical practice in the 1960s, and as their practice grew so did their support staff. Nurses, medical technicians, and office staff liked working there, and most remained on their jobs until they reached retirement age.

In the 1990s, Ethan, a third-generation Thompson, joined the practice just as his grandfather retired. As the patient load continued to grow, they brought in another doctor who seemed to fit in very well. After five years he asked to become a partner, his request was granted, and after following the necessary procedures he officially joined in the ownership of the practice.

But within a short period of time he started to bully the staff, actually reducing nurses to tears. The Drs. Thompson quickly spoke to their lawyer and were pleasantly surprised to learn that the dissolution of such medical partnerships was not uncommon and would not be a problem. Just as early intervention is crucial in early childhood bullying, so, too, is it important in workplace bullying.

Leadership, leadership, leadership . . . it's all about leadership, which in turn leads to good teamwork. Whether a small salon and spa tucked away on a beautiful Caribbean island or a major corporation in a bustling, major city on the mainland, the ingredients for a healthy, happy, productive workplace are the same. To reiterate Roshann's sage mantra, "A happy team begets great work . . .," the obvious goal of every workplace endeavor.

Chapter Seven

CYBER BULLYING:
PEER ABUSE IN ITS MOST LETHAL FORM

Cyber bullies maintain their anonymity by using fictitious names. Tim had invited several friends "to hang out at his house" one Sunday afternoon. As the group of high school freshmen was being picked up by their parents, a police car drove up. The officer said they had a report of cyber bullying that was coming from Tim's computer. The messages had been sent to Andrea, whose parents immediately reported it to the police, who in turn were able to trace them to Tim's computer. This took place in a very wealthy neighborhood, where the police department had state-of-the-art equipment. Probably the technology is similar to "Caller ID." Molly and Peggy had asked Tim earlier in the afternoon if they could use his computer. He'd said "sure," only to find that he had become their alias as they cyber bullied Andrea.

Tim's mother, who shared this story with me, told me she had been very upset by this episode on a number of counts: obviously, the fact that the girls had used her son's computer to cyber bully, that she always had thought Molly and Peggy were nice, sweet girls who turned out to be "mean girls," and that an afternoon she thought would be a good opportunity for her son to socialize with friends turned out the way it did.

Sameer Hinduja, Ph.D., and Justin W. Patchin, Ph.D., who conducted some of the earliest research on cyber bullying, define it as "willful and repeated harm inflicted through the medium of electronic text. Computers with Internet access and cellular phones are the primary ways through which bullying occurs."

The electronic devices have grown exponentially.

Discussions of cyber bullying have broadened under the heading of electronic bullying, which includes the use of electronic devices or the Internet to threaten, harass, embarrass, socially exclude, inflict emotional pain, and ruin reputations and friendships. Specific forms of electronic bullying include instant messaging (IM), texting, Twitter, e-mail, old-fashioned chat rooms, video clips via mobile phones, even websites.

Whereas a bully has traditionally needed some kind of physical or social advantage over his or her victim (physical or social stature or strength), the Internet has now paved the way for those with tech prowess to take advantage of those skills to bully others. This includes the short, geeky kid who more likely would have been the victim in the past.

What quickly comes to mind are the kids and adults sitting at their computers for hours, anonymously sending forth messages causing untold pain to countless victims of cyber bullying. Many cyber bully experts agree that a person who may never have had the power to bully face-to-face but is Internet-savvy can inflict a tremendous amount of pain upon another individual because of his or her IT prowess. In the Internet world people who are skilled on the computer, regardless of their physical stature, popularity, likeability, nerd reputation, and so on, can hold the power.

TYPES OF CYBER BULLYING

One can find stories about bullying as far back as Biblical days. If you Google "bullying in the Bible," you'll get thousands of hits. Electronic bullying/Cyber bullying has become the most recent form of this age-old source of human pain.

The complexity and reach of the Internet unfortunately allow for a wide variety of abuses to take place well beyond the realm of "traditional" bullying. And it is often difficult, if not impossible, to erase the widespread visibility of the harm done. Just like the old-fashioned bullying, cyber bullying occurs in many forms.

Following are some of the categories of cyber bullying:

Anonymity: The very nature of the Internet offers a wide cloak of anonymity to anyone who chooses to hide his or her identity. It enables the cyber bully to be completely unknown to the victim through the use of aliases or pseudonyms. One unfortunate victim of anonymous bullying, Jessica, a high school sophomore in a small Midwestern town, received hundreds of messages, sometimes on Facebook, other times by e-mail, that were so cruel they led to several attempts at suicide, leading up to her final, successful attempt. These messages were signed with names that meant nothing to her and seemed to come out of the blue. Jessica was an only child being raised by her single mother. Her mom moved them several times to neighboring communities, but the cyber bullying followed Jessica wherever they went. Jessica's story has, unfortunately, been repeated many times all over the world, not all ending in suicide, but causing an untold amount of pain. The messages as reported by the press worldwide seem very similar: "You are so ugly," "You should kill yourself," and "You don't deserve to live."

While Jessica received hundreds of messages signed with various unrecognizable names, Ella suddenly began receiving messages all signed *Jacqui*. She didn't know anyone by that name. Ella was an average middle school student with a nice group of friends and no known enemies, but the messages kept coming: Same messages in case after case: "You are so ugly." "You should kill yourself." Ella had no idea what prompted these messages, and after several years of relentless cyber bullying she also committed suicide.

Cyber stalking: Cyber stalking is considered a form of harassment. Targets like Donna begin to believe that the online cyber stalking might escalate to actual stalking. Donna and Sid, high school seniors, broke up after being together since freshman year. Sid began to cyber stalk Donna in the form of both e-mail and text messages, and she expressed concern that he would actually "live" stalk her. Although not all cyber stalking becomes live stalking, there are enough cases where it does that such a fear should be taken seriously.

Sometimes cyber stalking is just one point in a constellation of bullying experienced by a victim. In October 2012, ABC News reported that the YouTube video posted by Amanda Todd, a British Columbia teenager, had been viewed more than 17 million times. The title of her video was "My Story: Struggling, bullying, suicide, self-harm." Amanda's mother, Carol Todd, told the *Vancouver Sun*, "Every time she moved schools the cyber stalker would go undercover and become a Facebook friend."

Amanda hanged herself in her home on October 12, 2012, a little more than a month after she posted her story on YouTube, which many took to be a call for help.

Following the initial series of cyber bullying from a stranger on the Internet, which had led Amanda to perform actions that put her in jeopardy, Amanda experienced a domino effect of bullying that lasted several years and included abuse, bullying, cyber bullying, blackmail, harassment, and stalking online and in person. Although more than a million people clicked "Like" on Amanda's Memorial Facebook page, the "hate campaign" by others continued online even following her death.

The Royal Canadian Police and the British Columbia Coroner's Service conducted an extensive search for the perpetrator or perpetrators of Amanda's online torture. Two years later the BBC reported that Aydin Coban, a thirty-five-year-old man holding Dutch and Turkish citizenship, had been officially charged in the Netherlands in connection with Amanda's suicide. He was charged with extortion, Internet luring, criminal harassment, cyber stalking, live stalking, and child pornography. It appears he also had victims in the Netherlands, United Kingdom, and the United States. In January 2015 CBC News reported that Coban had written an open letter "professing his innocence." At this time no resolution of Amanda's case has been reported. There are several other suspects under investigation.

Once again, we learn about a tortured life and tragic death that continues to be repeated in so many countries worldwide. It is impossible to understand what possesses individuals to continue "hate campaigns" even after the cyber bullying victims have died. We must continue to combat hate with kindness.

Denigration: Denigration on the Internet is often referred to as online "dissing." The bully — student or adult — spreads rumors, lies, or gossip designed to hurt the victim's reputation. Among teenagers this is used as a vehicle to break up friendships and relationships. In the workplace, denigration can result in serious consequences for the victim's success or failure on the job.

A professor beloved by his students and colleagues was not given tenure at a midwestern university. The faculty committee was split, so the dean had to cast the deciding vote. After a careful review of the guidelines for granting tenure, he voted not to grant tenure.

Students launched a vicious cyber bullying campaign of denigration aimed at the dean. Day after day the students were online "dissing" their dean. Very much aware of the cyber bullying, which was relentless, the dean decided to call a meeting with the students, where a heated debate took place. Finally, one of the students who was a supporter of the dean's position turned to the leader of the opposition and said, "Stop bullying our dean." The dean had gone into great detail with me about his experience on campus with cyber bullying in general and his personal experience with denigration. He had a big smile as he repeated the student's comment, "Stop bullying our dean."

Exclusion: Exclusion is one of the most painful forms of bullying at any age. In the case of cyber bullying it is simply excluding someone from an online group and thereby causing the target a great deal of pain.

Exclusion has long been an issue in summer sleep-away camps. However, before the existence of the Internet, once the camp season was over, the bullying was also a matter of the past. Now the exclusion often continues year-round on the Internet.

In the workplace, victims are made aware of online groups and are sometimes cruelly taunted about being excluded. There are endless ways in which individuals are victims of exclusion in the workplace, including exclusion online.

Flaming: Flaming is a heated argument online through instant messaging or by e-mail. Offensive language is often used, as well as capital letters. Certainly, the highly publicized case of bullying by Miami Dolphins player Richie Incognito of his teammate Jonathan Martin included a tremendous amount of cyber bullying, much of it flaming. These were covered in great detail by the press from coast to coast. The offensive language going back and forth between the two players was shocking, and in the not-too-distant past would have been considered "not fit to print."

Harassment: Harassment occurs when messages of a threatening nature are posted online or sent to a target twenty-four hours a day. These messages are often posted on all sorts of social media.

Nellie worked at an upscale spa and endured verbal bullying abuse day after day from Corrine, the new office manager. Corrine questioned the products Nellie wanted to order for her clients, the appointments she made, and the hours she kept, even though Nellie had worked at the spa for twelve years. The harassment didn't stop when she came home at the end of her shift. It continued on into the evening and sometimes late into the night through e-mails and text messages from Corrine. Nellie finally decided it was not worth the emotional toll it was taking on her, and she quit. The owner of the spa finally fired Corrine after six months, but by that time more than ten longtime employees had also left.

Impersonation, masquerading, posing: The perpetrators of this type of cyber bullying go online as someone else with material and messages to get the person they're impersonating into trouble or, alternately, to get a third party in trouble. The messages or posts might put the victim in danger or damage his or her reputation. Many examples of this type of cyber bullying have been reported in the press when it has led to serious damage to reputations, friendships, and relationships, sometimes with consequences as serious as bullycide.

One of the most widely publicized cases of cyber bullying impersonation led to the case of the *United States Vs. Lori Drew*. Lori Drew was indicted on one count of conspiracy and three violations of the Computer Fraud and Abuse Act for accessing protected computers without authorization. With the help of her daughter, Sarah Drew, and Lori's eighteen-year-old employee Ashley Grills, Lori Drew set up an account on MySpace in the name of sixteen-year-old "Josh Evans" and contacted thirteen-year-old Megan Meier as Josh. "He" told Megan that his family had recently moved to neighboring O'Fallon, Missouri, that he was being home schooled and would like to be friends with her. He also told her that he had no phone, so she never spoke with him. Megan, who had weight issues and social problems, told her parents that this time of friendship with Josh made her happier than she'd ever been. After a little more than a month Josh's messages turned mean and cruel. His last message was, "The world would be a better place without you." Megan responded, "You are the kind of boy a girl would kill herself over." Twenty minutes after the last message, her mother found Megan in her bedroom closet where she had hanged herself.

The Drew and Meier families lived on the same street, four houses apart from one another. Sarah and Megan had been friends until something broke up their friendship. Lori Drew claimed that she perpetrated this hoax to find out information about Megan that she could later use to humiliate her in retaliation for what Lori believed she had done to her daughter, Sarah.

One can only wonder what would possess an adult to go to such lengths to interfere in a teenager's life. This tragedy devastated both families, had serious consequences for Ashley Grills, and negatively impacted some of the neighbors.

Outing: Outing is another form of cyber bullying that has taken a tremendous toll on its victims. It is the public display or forwarding of personal communication. It often involves sexual information that someone has shared with a friend with the belief that it will be held in the strictest of confidence. The most frequently used venues for outing are text messages, e-mail, and instant messaging. Outing has caused serious psychological damage and led to bullycide.

Tyler Clementi's story certainly shows us how outing can have tragic results.

Several other stories throughout the book introduce us to individuals who were victims of outing.

Trickery: Trickery is used to get someone to reveal secret information, which is then shared online. It is painful for the victim on two counts: first, because the individual feels betrayed by someone he thought could be trusted, and then because of the consequences brought about once the information has been made public.

Ryan Halligan was a thirteen-year-old special education student in Vermont. As is so often the case with special education students, Ryan unfortunately was the target of a great deal of bullying, especially by one boy. After a fight between the two boys in February 2003, it appeared that the bullying ended, and they became friends.

Soon after Ryan shared an embarrassing personal story with his new friend, the friend returned to his bullying ways and started a rumor online that Ryan was gay. Later that year Ryan's life met its tragic end, in bullycide.

Following Ryan's death his father found a folder of instant messages that clearly had inflicted enormous pain on his son. They were most painful for Mr. Halligan to read and made him realize "that technology was being used as weapons far more effective and far reaching (than) the ones we had as kids."

Many parents use being "technologically challenged" as an excuse for not keeping up with their children's lives online. This is no longer acceptable. The dangers involved with all types of bullying, but especially cyber bullying, require strict parental supervision of their children's online activities. Parents of young children should "learn as they go" with their children so they can be in step with their computer skills. Parents of older children should either ask their children to teach them how to use social media or find a computer expert to teach them. There are many computer classes and tutorials available, both online and in the classroom.

Following are some A-to-Z basics for protecting yourself and your children against cyber bullying:

- ***All*** bullying messages should be saved. They should not be deleted. These messages are important evidence of cyber bullying wherever it might take place.
- ***Before*** it even happens discuss the very serious dangers involved in cyber bullying with your children, students, or employees. Human Resources should be equipped to address cyber bullying in the workplace.
- ***Communicate*** the importance of NOT sharing personal information online with anyone. This includes name, address, phone number, pictures, e-mail address, and passwords. Also, very important to set one's privacy settings on Facebook (and perhaps other social media to select who sees what. We also need to keep up with managing our privacy settings since Facebook and other sites keep changing their parameters, which changes our privacy).
- ***Don't*** open messages from people you don't know — this is important for adults as well as children.
- ***Establish*** good communication with your children from early childhood on and keep those lines of communication open at all

times. It's important to establish good communication with your students and employees as quickly as possible.
- *Frequent* discussions with your children and students, or with your employees, are very important. Research has demonstrated the importance of ongoing dialogue on the topic of bullying from early childhood through senior adulthood.
- *Google* alerts should be set up in your child's name. Google is an excellent resource to help deal with any cyber bullying that might occur, as well as other forms of bullying.
- *Harassment* online can be reported by clicking "Help" or "Contact Us" when available by the provider or by submitting a complaint. When physical harm is threatened police should be notified.
- *Insist* on being kept informed about any cyber bullying activities your children and students might be experiencing. Human Resources should also be notified of any cyber bullying activities among employees. It is important for intervention to take place before the cyber bullying gets out of hand.
- Joel Haber's and Jena Glatzer's book, *Bullyproof Your Child for Life*, is a comprehensive guide for parents to "bullyproof" their children and contains very useful information on almost twenty websites that parents can use as resources to deal with cyber bullying.
- *Keep* track of **ALL** offensive messages. Stay abreast with cyber bullying developments as they occur.
- *Learn* as much as possible about your children's or students' world of social networking.
- *Many social networks* have security officers who try to take down offensive items in less than twenty-four hours. This is a vast improvement over earlier attempts to get items removed. During the early days of cyber bullying it would sometimes take months to have a post taken down. One example is of a Canadian mother who spent eight months trying to get false statements about her son removed, to no avail. The statements were out-and-out lies and were very hurtful. With improved vigilance today, that post would be removed within a day.
- *Networks*, such as Facebook and Twitter, all provide very clear

instructions on how to report abuses. (One way to find these instructions is to do a Google search such as "How do I report an abuse on [*name of Network*]?") Formspring advises users not to respond to mean comments, which will keep the comments from being seen by anyone else.
- **Offending messages** should be reported immediately.
- **Parents and school administrators** should contact police when children receive threatening messages. Adults should do the same when they receive threatening messages.
- **Quick**, thoughtful intervention is very important and very effective.
- **Resources** are available and should be used by parents, teachers, school administrators, Human Resources, and anyone in the position to help individuals who are the targets of bullies. These resources include books, videos, and presentations; many can be found online by Googling "bully prevention" or a specific book or video title.
- **School** resource officer is a school-based police officer who can also be contacted if a child receives threatening messages.
- **Teaching and modeling** kindness at all times are very powerful antidotes to bullying from early childhood through senior adulthood.
- **Understand** that bullying behavior is often "a call for help." Addressing this call could make an enormous difference in the life of a bully. All too often this is overlooked.
- **Very often** bullies are in pain and think that by inflicting pain on others they will lessen their own pain.
- **Witnesses** are key in the battle to banish bullying behavior. Teach children and students about the importance of choosing the witness role over the bystander role. The role of witnesses in the workplace is equally important. The witness might be able to get help before the bullying situation gets out of hand while the bystander does nothing.
- **Xenophobia** and other fears can cause some individuals to become bullies. They use their bullying behavior to cover up or mask their fears.

- ***Year-round*** efforts to banish bullying behavior are necessary to achieve success in the home, school, workplace, and senior adulthood communities.
- ***Zero tolerance*** for any type of bullying: cyber bullying, school yard bullying, sibling bullying, workplace and senior adulthood bullying.

With the advent of the Internet, bullying has taken on larger, more damaging proportions. Bullying now reaches more deeply into the private lives of the targets, and those of their families, following the victims from school or work into their own homes. The parents of the victims of bullycide have experienced an irretrievable loss, a hole that will never be filled. Yet, in the wake of the loss, many of these parents have become proactive in trying to prevent further incidents of cyber bullying and bullycide. Their wish is for other children not to have to endure the emotional pain their children experienced, and for other parents not to suffer the devastating loss they've suffered.

Joseph and Jane Clementi founded the Tyler Clementi Foundation in memory of their son "out of the urgent need to address the needs of vulnerable populations, especially LGBT and other victims of hostile social environments." It has a very active board of directors, as well as a professional staff. The foundation provides education about online and offline bullying, resources for victims and targets, and contact information for suicide support and prevention. More specifics about the outstanding work of the foundation will be discussed in Chapter Ten.

Tina Meier is the director of the Megan Meier Foundation. She estimates that she has reached approximately 140,000 people with her talks to students and adults during the first six years following Megan's death. Her message to students is to be kind to each other, more aware of how their words can hurt, and to seek help when they need it.

John and Kelly Halligan established a foundation in memory of their son, Ryan. Their foundation focuses on "prevention, presentations, and resources," and they have shared their message throughout the United States, Canada, and Latin America. Within a short time after his son died John spearheaded the passage of the Vermont Bully Prevention Bill in May 2004. Two years later, in April 2006, he worked to pass a law pertaining to Mandatory Suicide Prevention education in public schools.

These parents and the parents of many other victims of bullycide desperately want to keep the memories of their children alive. They also want us to join them in their call to action, which I'll discuss in greater detail in Chapter Ten.

Chapter Eight

FROM PEER ABUSE TO ELDER ABUSE

At a hearing in 2011 of the Senate Special Committee on Aging, Mickey Rooney described what it felt like to be financially exploited. "You can be in control of your life one minute, and in the next minute, you have absolutely no control. In my case, I was eventually and completely stripped of the ability to make even the most basic decisions in my life . . . If elder abuse happened to me, Mickey Rooney, it can happen to anyone. Myself, who I am, what I hope to be, and what I was, was taken from me. And I am asking you [Congress] to stop this NOW."

According to one estimate, one million older Americans lose $2.6 billion annually as a result of financial abuse. And this is just one type of elder abuse that goes on. Elder abuse, also known as *senior adult bullying*, is far more common than most would guess. You may be surprised to learn that ten to twenty percent of senior adults are bullied in senior living communities, assisted living facilities, senior centers, and nursing homes. It's harder to quantify the number of seniors bullied in their own homes, in the home of a family member or friend, or by their adult children, caregivers, or neighbors.

The definition for senior bullying is very similar to the general definition of bullying: It is intentional repetitive behavior that hurts another person, physically or mentally. It involves an imbalance of power, strength, or mental fitness and often involves issues of control.

When thinking of elder abuse, most of us conjure images of caregivers or other young people taking advantage of elders. Although this is often the case, there are other scenarios of elder abuse where the bully is a senior adult him- or herself. Any setting where groups of elders live or spend time together is a potential setting for bullying to occur.

Among senior adults, however, there is a caveat when it comes to identifying bullying behaviors. What looks like abuse or bullying can sometimes instead indicate underlying issues of dementia or other mental health problems. Therefore, these issues need to be ruled out by a qualified professional.

TYPES OF ELDER ABUSE

As we know, many senior adults live in assisted living facilities or retirement homes; others who still live independently or with their adult children participate in daytime activities sponsored by community centers or social service agencies. Programs include classes in a variety of subjects such as art, music, and bridge. There are often field trips to museums, concerts, sightseeing, and the like. Most programs also include a hot lunch. The setting at these facilities is reminiscent of the childhood backdrop for group interaction — classroom, school bus, and cafeteria — and just like those childhood settings, they can provide the perfect storm for bullying to erupt.

Bullying can occur among seniors in many of the same ways it does among their younger counterparts — when a bossy senior adult tells others where to sit on the bus or at the lunch table, when an established group of friends does not allow someone new to join them at a craft table, when cruel words are aimed at a person in front of others, or even when physical force is used. Whatever the type of bullying, it's a painful experience for the target. Following is a discussion of the various types of bullying that can show up in senior adult settings.

PHYSICAL ABUSE

Maurice is still an imposing six-foot-two figure at age 83. He was big even as a child, and he is still used to throwing his weight around. When he doesn't get his way, he won't hesitate to push and shove his target. On more than one occasion he has knocked down a fellow senior adult. The professional staff at the retirement community where he and his wife live, intervenes, the physical bullying stops for a few days, and then Maurice returns to the same bullying behavior. Maurice owned a construction company and did not hesitate to bully his employees. Business was good; the pay was good, so the employees put up with his bullying. Over the years a few employees left because of the bullying but far less than one would expect.

Physical abuse includes hitting, beating, pushing, shaking, kicking, destroying property, and stealing. Some have even reported burning.

Although physical bullying is much less prevalent among senior adults than it is during childhood, the threat of physical abuse can be wielded as effectively by a senior adult bully as physical abuse itself. However, the bully who stole his classmates' lunch money might carry his stealing tactics with him all through his life and take them into a senior residential facility. This would be an example of bullying that did not get interrupted by early intervention ("once a bully, always a bully").

VERBAL ABUSE

Daphne was a "mean girl" in middle school, and she continues to intimidate, humiliate, and ridicule other senior adult women who participate in the same senior adult daytime program she does. "Bessie, how can you wear such an ugly outfit?" she can be heard yelling across the room. Of course, Bessie's face turns bright red in embarrassment. On another occasion, she tells Joanne, "If you don't let me sit there, I won't let you sit at our table at lunch." One could easily mistake this for a middle school scene.

Verbal abuse includes intimidation through yelling and/or threats, name-calling, humiliation, scapegoating, ridicule, insults, or any type of hurtful language.

EMOTIONAL ABUSE

Emotional elder abuse behaviors also include many of the same bullying behaviors at play among the "mean girls" in grade school. Exclusion is one of the most painful forms of emotional abuse from early childhood all the way through senior adulthood. It doesn't matter that a senior adult has acquired a lifetime of experience and wisdom; exclusion and other emotional abuse still cut just as deep.

Much like the bullying in middle school lunchrooms and workplace dining rooms, plenty of exclusion takes place in the dining halls of senior adult facilities. This was what happened to Emma. A fellow resident of an assisted living facility told Emma that she was not welcome to sit at her table anymore. The social worker attempted to work with Tricia, the bully, but to no avail. As happens all too often in senior settings, the other residents, some who were actually Emma's friends, were afraid to intervene. Emma was hesitant to try to sit at a different table for fear of being rejected once again. She became more and more isolated, staying in her room a great deal of the time. The social worker tried to convince Emma that she was not the problem, that the bully was the problem, again to no avail.

Emma's children became concerned about their mother's inability to cope with the situation and investigated a number of other senior living facilities. They met with the social worker in each one, explained their mother's situation, and chose the facility in which they thought their mother would have the best professional and peer support system. Their choice proved to be an excellent one, and Emma became an integral member of her new retirement community.

Emma's story is an important one on a number of levels. Keeping in mind that ten to twenty percent of the residents of senior residential facilities are bullied, it is imperative to check out how the professional staff addresses this important issue. The social environment created by the administration, staff, and residential community should be a high priority in the evaluation of any senior living facility.

Emma had never been bullied before, and she still hasn't figured out what made her a target this late in life. What we do know is that appropriate professional intervention is just as important to resolving peer abuse among elders as it is among children and teens in school and camp settings.

In addition to exclusion, emotional abuse also includes ignoring, isolating, shunning, spreading rumors, gossiping, negative body language, rude gestures, mimicking, rolling one's eyes, and other demeaning facial expressions.

SEXUAL ABUSE

Only about thirty percent of senior sexual abuse is reported, which makes this a hidden problem in many senior living facilities, as well as in other senior living situations. At one high-income senior city community center, an attendant forced several women into sexual activity for many months. None of them reported the abuse to authorities. However, a relative of one of the victims became suspicious that something was wrong when he saw bruises on his mother, and she told her son about the physical force an attendant used to get her "to cooperate." Her son immediately reported the abuse, and of course the perpetrator was fired.

Sexual abuse includes sexual touching, showing pornographic material, molestation, rape, sex acts, and any forced or coerced sexual activity.

As reported in May 2013 by the Pennsylvania Coalition Against Rape, 83.3 percent of senior sexual abuse occurs in nursing homes or other adult care facilities, and 26.8 percent in the family home. Eighty-one percent of the perpetrators are caregivers. Other perpetrators include fellow residents and family members, including spouses.

With the small percentage of elder sexual abuse cases being reported there is very sketchy statistical reporting. Statistic Brain Database reports an average each year of 2,150,000 cases of elder sexual abuse 67.3 percent of the victims are women, and 32.7 percent are men. On the other hand, the Department of Health and Human Services' Administration for Community Living reports that 93.2 percent of the victims are women, and 6.8 percent are men. The average age of the victims is about seventy-eight years.

FINANCIAL ABUSE

Financial abuse is defined by Brayton Purcall, LLP, as "the improper use of an elder's funds, property or assets." Attorneys have found that the perpetrators of financial abuse include family members, friends, caregivers, or someone who holds power of attorney, as well as financial institutions.

Mickey Rooney's tragic story certainly illustrates the financial abuse all too many senior adults experience. Dr. Smith, a retired physician who had cared for many senior adult patients, told me, "You would not believe how badly some adult children treat their elderly parents. It broke my heart to observe what these people endured in their old age. It was abundantly clear to me that many of the children were eager for their parents to die so they could collect their inheritance!"

Dr. Smith continued to make house calls for his elderly patients long after most physicians had discontinued that practice. In one case he found an elderly couple "held hostage by their psychotic daughter," he told me. This couple had been his patients for over thirty years, and he found them sleeping on cots in the living room of their million-dollar home. In their eighties, they were not properly fed nor cleaned. Neighbors complained that the property was not maintained, and the house was in disrepair. Their daughter was incapable of taking care of herself or her parents. Dr. Smith called in state social services, but he told me "they blew it." They just didn't provide the intervention needed by this family. Sad to hear about prominent members of the community ending their days in this way.

This was not an isolated case, and every physician in every field of medicine confirmed that they see elder abuse among their patients both those cared for at home and those in retirement centers. They all say, "It is just awful."

Recently a local Kansas City TV news anchor interviewed a World War II highly decorated, including Purple Heart, veteran who had his life savings of $69,000 stolen from one account and $24,000 from another account. The perpetrators are a husband and wife whom he hired to help with the day-to-day homemaking chores after his wife died. They conned him into giving them access to his accounts so they could pay his bills.

He wore his army uniform during the interview and looked much younger than his ninety years. He was articulate as he shared his tragic story. He finally told a younger friend at church about his financial losses, and this friend is helping to track the couple on the run. Our vet is very concerned that the couple might come after him.

According to the Consumer Law Center, Inc. (CLC), Americans lose an estimated $40 billion each year to telephone scams. Senior citizens are often the targets of this fraudulent telemarketing, with between fifty-six percent to nearly eighty percent of their calls made to this part of our population. One sweepstakes-related scam reported on CBS's "60 Minutes" bilked seniors in twenty-four states out of an estimated $5 billion!

NEGLECT

Neglect occurs when seniors don't receive proper amounts of food, water, clothing, shelter, medications, care for their physical needs and cleanliness, and assurance of personal safety. More than half the cases of elder abuse are related to some form of neglect.

Dr. Jones divorced his wife of thirty-five years to marry a young nurse who worked in his office. He was a severe diabetic and had to retire early. Friends and colleagues noticed that he was losing weight and that his wife was not giving him insulin as needed. It was clear that his wife was guilty of serious neglect.

Dr. Smith called to invite Dr. Jones to lunch. His wife never gave him the message, and when Dr. Smith arrived to pick up his friend at noon, he found him still in his pajamas, his blood sugar level at a dangerous high of 600, and his wife gone for the day.

Dr. Smith told me that Dr. Jones's friends literally kidnapped him so his wife would not know where he was and took him to a friend's home who nursed Dr. Jones in her home and then made arrangements for him to move into a nursing home, where he received excellent care. Although it was not a romantic relationship, it was a long and abiding friendship, and she actually visited him every day of the week and kept him company all day until Dr. Jones died.

As we have traced bullying behaviors through the various stages of childhood and adulthood, we have seen that some types of bullying are the same throughout and other types are somewhat different at various stages. One of the bullying behaviors described in early childhood is "bossiness," as opposed to bullying, which does not appear again until senior adulthood! For no apparent reason, bossiness is not considered bullying at other stages of life.

Although some senior adult bullies have exhibited bullying behavior since childhood, others have only begun to bully at this stage in their lives. The latter appear to be people who feel they are losing control of their lives and therefore try to exert control over others. Some are individuals who held a lot of power throughout their adult years and are trying to regain that sense of power through bullying.

As is often the case with younger bullies, senior bullies can be individuals who have difficulties in social relationships. Many bullies of all ages lack empathy. They may have low self-esteem and build themselves up by putting others down.

Antisocial behavior and social aggression are common forms of bullying in the social setting of living facilities. A key to creating a healthy environment for senior adults is a staff that is well-trained and skilled at appropriate intervention in these situations. Research has shown that if intervention does not take place quickly the situation only escalates.

SENIOR ADULTHOOD RESPONSES TO BULLYING

Depending on the setting, senior adults respond to bullying in a variety of ways. Whether at home or in a senior living environment, elders may become depressed, experience anxiety or frustration, might consider suicide, become angry, change their eating and sleeping habits, and experience increased physical problems or an exacerbation of mental health issues.

Elders often experience lower self-esteem as part of the aging process, which can intensify as the result of being bullied. They may retaliate and then feel ashamed. In a senior living facility or day facility when residents are not welcomed at a dining table or card game, they often start to isolate themselves. This might occur when rumors have been spread about them or they know they are the objects of gossip.

Family members, caregivers, and professional staff must be alerted to changes in the behavior of senior adults and the possibility that bullying and elder abuse could be a factor. It is imperative that immediate, appropriate intervention takes place.

In a senior living facility, there are bound to be witnesses to bullying incidents. As in younger bullying situations, witnesses experience a variety of reactions. Some are afraid they will be the next target and actually join in the attack to try to prevent being targeted, some feel guilty for not intervening, and others may experience a feeling of helplessness. Then there are the senior adults who are defenders, those who are confident enough to come to the aid of the target by standing up to the bullies and telling them to stop. Other defenders take action by immediately reporting the situation to the proper authority for intervention.

CREATING A BULLY-FREE ENVIRONMENT

Senior adults have every right to expect that they will live in a bully-free environment when they move into their senior living facility. The administration and staff should create an atmosphere in which each member feels warmly welcomed and an integral part of a vibrant community — a community in which its members really care about one another, show respect for each other, and are kind in their words and actions. The result of creating such an environment is that individuals living there have a feeling of belonging and being connected to others; they feel cared about and are able to contribute to the community.

Senior adults in community living situations should be taught how to resolve conflicts, which are bound to arise in relatively close living quarters. When conflict arises a qualified staff member should be right on top of the situation. It should not be necessary for the target to have to cope with the bullying behavior on his or her own. However, many social workers in senior settings maintain that it's also important for elders to have general coping skills that will stand them in good stead should they be faced with a bullying situation. They recommend that elders be taught to:

- Stand their ground;
- Indicate they are not looking for conflict and would prefer friendship;
- Be clear that they do not want to participate in gossip (gossip is an emotionally painful form of elder abuse);
- Make a real effort to be part of the community;
- Talk to a "trusted adult," family member, friend, staff, clergy, or doctor;
- Recognize when they've made a mistake, learn from it, and move on;
- Train themselves to have a positive outlook;
- Try not to overreact to stressful situations;
- Try to be objective, to address situations thoughtfully rather than

emotionally (when a situation is addressed emotionally the emotion becomes the focus instead of the actual problem);
- Accept responsibility for their own actions but not to assume the responsibility of others.

It is important also to teach senior adults in a community setting how to support and defend each other in potential bullying situations. In other words, they should learn how to become defenders rather than bystanders. There are a number of responses available to a witness that would allow him or her to become a defender:
- Intervening by physically moving next to the target to indicate support, speaking up, or telling the bully to stop;
- Reporting the episode to the proper authorities so they can intervene quickly;
- Bringing humor into the situation, which has been used effectively by students and adults I have worked with.

One example of humor coming to the rescue can be found in Mimi's story. Mimi had a severe allergic reaction to a new medication. She broke out in a rash all over her body, including her face, which looked like teenage acne. John started calling her "pizza face" for days on end, which made her feel even worse about the situation. Tony, Mimi's significant other, finally turned to John and asked, "What flavor would you like today, cheese, veggie, or sausage?" This received a good laugh from the crowd and stopped the bullying. It works every time!

If all of these guidelines are followed for creating a harmonious environment, many potential problems will be averted. But in any situation involving group dynamics, there are bound to be at least occasional incidents, and the administration needs to be prepared to deal with them.

We must especially be mindful of those individuals who are in the "once a bully, always a bully" category. During interviews with professionals, administrators and staff members of senior living facilities, they told me that when they discuss the bullying behaviors with the adult children of the perpetrators, they are often told, "Oh, my mother/father bullied me all my life. Do you really think I can change the behavior now?" These situations require professional intervention by a geriatric social worker and/or psychologist also trained to work with the elderly. If the bully does not respond to the intervention his/her adult children might be asked to move their parent to another facility. Sometimes the threat of a move will be a "wake-up call" for the bully, and at other times, sadly, the bully will have to be moved a number of times.

LEGAL PROTECTION FOR ELDERS

Similar to the case of child abuse legislation, there is great variation from state to state with proposed laws to protect senior adults from elder abuse. However, legislatures in all fifty states have passed some forms of elder abuse prevention laws. Quite a few states have implemented mandatory reporting, yet elder abuse remains widely under-reported. It will take the combined efforts of both criminal justice officials and social services staff to assure that the laws have the necessary impact and effect for which they are intended.

There is help available at www.HelpGuide.org for senior adults and/or their family members. Once you have reached the website, click on "How to spot the warning signs of elder abuse." There you will find a wealth of in-depth information including the following topics:

- What is elder abuse?
- Different types
- Signs and symptoms
- Risk factors
- Prevention
- Reporting
- Reporting abuse in the home
- More help
- Resources and references — including helplines and hotlines

It is imperative for senior adults to report any type of abuse to their family members, friends, or qualified professionals so the abuse is stopped. Experience has shown that the longer abuse or bullying continues the worse it will get.

SABRINA

Sabrina is one of the most extraordinary people I know. Seventy-five friends and relatives between the ages of twenty and ninety-five recently feted her at her one hundredth birthday luncheon celebration. Without exaggeration, at the age of one hundred she looks like a young seventy-year-old, her blond hair perfectly coiffed, her elegant outfit just right for her trim figure, the twinkle in her eyes, and a smile that lights up a room.

Sabrina, a Conservatory of Music graduate was a concert pianist until she started her family. She continues to play an hour every day and perform at social functions. In addition, she has a university degree in social work and pursued a career in that field while raising her family. Her third career was in the world of fashion as a personal shopper in an upscale boutique.

Sabrina and I belong to several of the same community organizations, and when she heard via the grapevine that I was writing a book about bullying she invited me to lunch at her retirement community to share her experience with bullies in first grade.

As I entered the main building, I was struck by the fact that I wasn't in a lobby but rather I had entered directly into a living room with a fireplace, comfortable seating arrangements, and a large baby grand piano.

Sabrina greeted me warmly and led me to the café where residents entertain guests for meals.

Sabrina's father came to the United States from Russia in the late 1920s and when he had a job, he arranged for his family to join him. Sabrina arrived in her new homeland in 1932, two days before school started. She did not know one word of English. As she walked to school in the new dress her father had bought her, some boys behind her started to yell at her. She had no idea what they were saying, so did not react. They shoved her and pushed her to the ground. The bullies had demanded that she move aside, and when she didn't react, they resorted to physical bullying.

Sabrina's next-door neighbor was a classmate and became her protector against bullies. She taught Sabrina English, and they were lifelong friends.

The fact that Sabrina felt it was important for her to share her bully story with me after all these decades and such a full life should speak volumes to all of us. She is truly an inspiration to many people who know her.

The opportunity to visit with Sabrina in her adult retirement community both for the interview and her birthday celebration enabled me to see what a continued care community really encompasses. They are set on beautifully landscaped campuses and include freestanding houses for independent living, assisted living apartments, skilled nursing and memory care. Many of these communities belong to a nationwide network, and when you call to inquire, you speak to a senior living advisor who will match you, potential resident, with the appropriate community.

What impressed me most about Sabrina's community was how happy everyone she introduced me to seemed to be. Several people just said straightforward they were so happy to be living in this community. Everything about it, the people, the programs, the food, the care as needed, really everything a retirement community should be to make the golden years truly golden. As we continue to learn more and more about elder abuse, we should be able to keep the bullies at bay and seniors safe.

Here we have yet another call for action to protect the ten to twenty percent of our elders who are the targets and victims of bullying behaviors in senior settings.

Chapter Nine

KINDNESS: AN ANTIDOTE FOR BULLYING BEHAVIOR

*"There are three things in life that are important
The first is to be kind.
The second is to be kind.
The third is to be kind."*

— Henry James

As painful as Andrew's bullying memories are, he also has fond memories of being the recipient of numerous acts of kindness. Several of his classmates' parents invited him to their homes for dinner and in some instances to spend the weekend.

Andrew could turn on the charm around adults, even at a very young age. He was good looking and intelligent, and none of the parents believed that he was "the bully" so many of his classmates described. They also felt sorry for him because of his parents' divorce and the pain that caused in his young life.

Although these acts of kindness relieved the pain he felt for a short time, it soon returned "full force." As we learned from Andrew, his decades of bullying were based on a very complex set of circumstances.

Nevertheless, one of the antidotes for bullying behavior is kindness.

There are many facets of kindness such as modeling, promoting, and enjoying, just to mention a few. Ryan's story is a wonderful example of the powerful effect of modeling kindness.

Ryan, a young Red Sox fan, demonstrated several facets of kindness for the whole world to see. As the 2014 baseball season was winding down, one of the most heartwarming stories was televised from Fenway Park in Boston. Twelve-year-old Ryan was handed a foul ball on the third base line by one of the team's ball girls. Ryan immediately turned around and gave the ball to a shocked but delighted little girl sitting behind him. Jerry Remy, Red Sox announcer on NESN, said, "I think that's one of the nicest things I have seen in the ballpark all year."

Ryan was interviewed live and said, "I've seen people do it before, and I thought it was a nice thing, and it's nice to make people happy." When asked by Gary Striewski during the interview how many people he thought saw his "act of kindness" on TV, Ryan shrugged and said, "maybe 10,000." Based on the number of newspapers alone that carried the story, the figure goes well into the millions. Add to that the story's appearance on television and the Internet, Ryan's act of kindness was witnessed by additional millions of people. Just as Ryan saw kindness modeled when he watched ball games, hopefully many others will remember Ryan's "act of kindness" and follow suit, whether they're at a ball game or they're faced with a decision about what behavior is appropriate in their day-to-day lives. Ryan's story reminds us of how powerful acts of kindness can be.

From Boston we moved to Philadelphia, and from the baseball field to the workplace, from a school-age boy to an adult who both modeled kindness. Their actions promoted kindness and demonstrated how both Ryan and Mara enjoyed their "acts of kindness."

Mara took an entry-level job with the City of Philadelphia right after she graduated with a BA from the University of Pennsylvania. She was "testing the waters" to explore whether she wanted to pursue a career in urban planning. Mara found her boss, Sophia, to be "one big bully." Mara looked for sympathy from anyone who would listen.

"Why do I have to suffer whenever she is having a bad day? I know the minute she walks into the office by her body language whether I'm in for a bad day as well."

After many months of this, one of Mara's friends suggested she try an entirely different approach. "Remember how they taught us at school that 'kindness is contagious — catch it?' Why don't you try it? You have nothing to lose."

Mara decided to take the suggestion and run with it. Rather than simply being kind to her boss, she decided to be kind to everyone in the office and really spread it around. She baked a couple of batches of chocolate chip cookies, prepared a baggie of cookies for each person in her office including her boss, tied each bag with a bow, and attached a little note, "To sweeten your day." Much to their delight each of her colleagues found a baggie on his or/her desk. This simple "act of kindness" was the beginning of many creative "acts of kindness" that had a lasting effect on Mara's workplace.

Sally made a "Bull's Eye Chart," a poster with a bull's eye in the center and concentric circles around it. Everyone was invited to use "Post-its" to write something positive about their colleagues, i.e. "I love Sam's sense of humor," "Way to go Emma," or "Great job on the project, Tom." I have used this "Bull's Eye Chart" in many settings: with undergraduate students and graduate students at the university, at conferences, both professional and volunteer, and in the workplace with the same success Sally experienced. It is a very simple way to encourage colleagues to look for the positive characteristics in each other.

Louis, who was known for his culinary skills, organized a "potluck" lunch that was so successful they decided to have one each month with a different theme.

Mara's boss still had "bad days," but they were few and far between. She even came up with her own version of the chocolate chip cookies baggies! Turned out that Sophia made wicked good fudge! Mara's simple "act of kindness" brought about total change in the environment of her office and her ability to cope with her boss's moods.

MANY FACETS OF KINDNESS

The power of kindness cannot be overstated. It is most effective to prevent bullying before it starts but can also be very effective when bullying occurs. When I asked the director of an early childhood center if I could interview her for my first book, her answer was, "We don't have any bullying. We teach kindness." Several years later she called me to tell me that they had had their first problem with a young bully, they made a referral for professional psychological intervention, and within a matter of a few months this child's problems were addressed and the bullying behavior banished. Bullying behavior can often be a call for help and with professional attention and intervention can be eliminated.

Mara's experience is just one example of how the power of kindness transformed one workplace environment. It's a topic that brought forth countless stories and "aha moments" during discussions which I had with both children and adults during interviews for this book. In addition to the one-on-one interviews, I conducted several workshops for both children and adults, and in each workshop one story would remind someone of a long-forgotten "act of kindness" by a parent or grandparent, by a classmate or beloved teacher. There were stories about finding loving notes in lunch boxes or in camp duffel bags, kind words to heal the wounds of a nasty encounter or a disappointing loss at a sports event.

Modeling kindness starts in the home and is very effective in early childhood education and throughout school years. It is an obvious way for parents, childcare providers, grandparents, and everyone who touches the life of the child to communicate the efficacy of kindness at a very early age. All adults should use every opportunity to model kindness.

Educators who **teach** kindness report that they do not have a problem with student bullying. **Modeling** and **teaching** kindness should be an integral part of the school day, as well as life at home and the workplace. Ryan's story reminds us of the positive effect that modeling can have on young children. The young child who quietly helped her friend who had an "accident" in class has had kindness modeled in her home from the time she was born. When a new mom is overwhelmed with the twenty-four/seven tasks of motherhood, someone has had a death in the family, or is taking chemo treatments, her mom is the first to arrange a meal schedule for friends and family to prepare food to ease the burdens. Her dad is the "go-to guy" for car pools and team coaching.

Modeling kindness is equally important in the workplace. Modeling kindness starts at the top and is just as important at every level of management.

The simple act of offering your seat to an elderly person on the bus or subway can serve as a model for those witnessing it, and possibly, they will do the same thing the next time an opportunity arises.

Apply acts of kindness at every opportunity. Ryan's baseball story is an excellent example of modeling kindness; it also illustrates taking the opportunity to apply an act of kindness in a given situation.

Think back on the various stories of kindness in earlier chapters, and you will note how individuals applied acts of kindness given the opportunity.

Know kindness. One can know kindness by experiencing it. One experience I have had of knowing kindness was when our phone rang at 3 a.m. the morning we were to catch a very early plane. Our alarm clock was ringing at the same time. I couldn't begin to imagine who would be calling us at that time. It turned out to be my ninety-five-year-old dad, who had set *his* alarm to call us to make sure we did not oversleep! As the recipient of his "act of kindness" I was reminded of all the acts of kindness my dad had modeled for us throughout his entire life and that one is never too old to model kindness.

Both the recipient of the act of kindness and the individual who performs it can enjoy kindness. When children in the classroom, at scout meetings, and other social activities were invited by me to share stories about acts of kindness they had received, they were often surprised by how many there have been and how much they enjoyed them. When adults were invited to do so at workshops and social functions, they had a very similar reaction. By the same token, when I gave them the opportunity to share experiences about the acts of kindness they themselves had performed, they were also surprised and pleased to realize the pleasure they had had from doing so.

Jet Express is a perfect example of **enjoying kindness.** It is a program to help people over the age of sixty-five to stay active and independent even if they can no longer drive. Volunteers drive these senior citizens to medical appointments, the grocery store, and hairdressers. Many of the volunteers drive the same person to weekly appointments. Long-lasting friendships develop by both the recipients and volunteers who share these acts of kindness.

Bev, the executive director of a not-for-profit organization, became a Jet Express volunteer in 2012. She takes an extended lunch hour once a week to drive ninety-four-year-old Sara to her church for her exercise class! While Sara exercises, Bev, who is in her fifties, runs errands for Sara: groceries, CVS, meds for her dog from her vet, and the like. When she brings Sara home Bev will do a few chores around the house and then return to her office. Needless to say, Bev and Sara have established a strong bond and exemplify the enjoyment of kindness by both the individual performing the act of kindness and the recipient of that act of kindness. Sara knit a beautiful scarf for Bev last year.

"Sara and I clicked the moment we met," Bev told me.

In addition to the practical aspect of the program, Jet Express provides transportation for senior citizen Saturday night dating and other social functions.

Jan and Alex became "an item" after their spouses passed away when they were in their eighties. When Alex's health issues made it necessary for him to move into a senior citizen facility about ten miles from where Jan lives, and neither of them can drive any longer, Alex at age ninety-five is still able to take his sweetheart out to dinner on Saturday night, thanks to Jet Express.

Nurturing kindness is an ongoing process for young and old alike. Kindness should be encouraged and rewarded for both young and old, day in and day out. A smile and kind word can be an ample reward for most people.

Professor Christine Porath conducted an experiment in which a smile and simple thanks (as compared with not doing this) resulted in people being viewed as twenty-seven percent warmer, thirteen percent more competent, and twenty-two percent more civil. This certainly underscores the efficacy of the most basic forms of encouraging and rewarding acts of kindness by those who participated in the study.

Acknowledge kindness whenever you have the opportunity to do so. Communicate that kindness is an expected behavior. Kindness can be acknowledged verbally or with a warm smile, as Dr. Porath's study demonstrated.

I find it especially heartwarming when a young person opens or holds open a door for me. It brings a smile to my face and a "Thank you so much" to my lips.

Promoting kindness can take place by acknowledging, modeling, and teaching kindness. The very acts of acknowledging, modeling, and teaching kindness promote kindness. Each and all of these actions are powerful vehicles to promote kindness. Each in its own way enables us to promote kindness.

For example, a citywide student essay contest to nominate several people for being kind is a method for teaching kindness and also promotes kindness. Impartial judges read the thousands of essays, and then winning essays are read by their authors at a "Kindness Dinner" at which they introduce their nominees. Over the years the winners have included an elderly school street crossing guard and a quarterback on the Kansas City Chiefs, to give you an idea of the broad range of nominees and winners.

The essay contest is an excellent opportunity for teaching kindness in the classroom, and the dinner is an equally excellent opportunity to promote kindness to the whole community.

Envision kindness is an integral part of everyday life — at home, at school, at play, and in the workplace. Be creative and let yourself be inspired by those around you who have not only envisioned kindness but have implemented practices in their lives or organizations. Ochsner Health System, a large health care provider in Louisiana, implemented the "ten/five way" in which employees are encouraged to make eye contact within ten feet of someone and say hello within five feet. They report positive effects on both their employees and their clientele. Many children would also enjoy the "10/5 way."

One of the most inspiring acts of kindness that I observed was during a visit to a pre-kindergarten preschool class. Katie and Beth were painting at their easels, side by side. Suddenly Katie noticed that Beth had had "an accident," wet her pants, probably because she was so engrossed in her artwork! Katie quietly walked to her cubby, took out her extra pair of panties, took Beth by the hand, and together they walked to the girl's room, got Beth into dry, clean panties, and resumed painting.

Celebrate kindness by sharing it. Remember, "Kindness is contagious — catch it." Kindness is celebrated at an annual fundraising dinner honoring five civic leaders for their acts of kindness. Each honoree is asked to share a brief story about an act of kindness of which he/she was the recipient. Listening to these women and men who are community leaders share their stories of kindness received always is very inspiring. The dinner is a celebratory evening and also promotes kindness.

The newscasters at Fenway Park were certainly celebrating Ryan's act of kindness with their effusive reporting of his story. These topics can be discussed at home, around the dinner table, in the classroom, and in the workplace during weekly or monthly team meetings.

Participants in these discussions might share remembrances of how they were taught about kindness as children and how they taught kindness as adults: as parents, teachers, social workers, and members of the workforce.

KINDNESS DEFINED

Usually one defines a term at the outset of the discussion. However, I wanted to give you the opportunity to define kindness for yourself before giving you the generally accepted definitions. If you haven't yet come up with your own definition, take a moment now, before you read the definitions, to do just that. You can use these questions to guide your thinking about it:

- What is kindness?
- What does it mean to be kind?
- How does kindness look in action?
- How does it make you feel to be the recipient of a kind act?
- How does it make you feel to be the one *being* kind?
- To whom do you want to be kind?

These questions can be used to promote a discussion about kindness at home, in school, or at the workplace.

Here are the generally accepted dictionary definitions:
- Showing sympathy, empathy, understanding
- Charitable, humane
- Friendly, generous, warm-hearted

- To be mindful of others
- To be equally nice to everyone, including pets
- Have a good or benevolent nature or disposition

Again, the power of kindness can't be underestimated in our work to prevent bullying behavior and in our response to it. Small acts of kindness can make a big difference. This should be kept in mind at all times as we address the serious epidemic of bullying behavior.

Chapter Ten

MODEL RESPONSES TO THE CALL FOR ACTION

Preston Kitchen, a tall, thin eighth-grader, who played both violin and football, was the ongoing target of a much larger bully from the same grade. The bully, who weighed 200 pounds, threatened Preston in the hallways, tripped him in gym class, and dumped food on him in the cafeteria, to the point that Preston would not go to his locker to retrieve his violin for fear of yet another attack.

Preston's mother reported this to the school, and both boys "got a talking to," but the bullying continued. Preston told his mother that he didn't think the lecture by the principal had done any good. It was like a scene from the documentary film "Bully," where the principal gives the bully and victim a "talking to," and it is clear that nothing positive is happening.

Preston's grandfather sent a certified letter to the principal, "imploring the school authorities to step in 'with discretion for fear of revenge.'" However, matters got worse when the bully attacked Preston's younger brother, twelve-year-old Blake, which hospitalized the sixth-grader for five days. At the time, Blake was four feet, six inches tall and weighed seventy-four pounds. The bully — more than twice Blake's weight and a foot taller, smashed Blake's head into the cafeteria table, punched him in the face, and body-slammed him to the floor. This knocked Blake unconscious, leaving him bleeding, with a broken jaw, fractured skull, and cerebrospinal fluid leaking from one ear. The attack left him with a hearing loss and balance issues due to inner ear damage.

The Liberty, Missouri, School District reported the case to the police department, who carried out a thorough investigation. The district was cooperating with law enforcement. Following the investigation, the case was turned over to the Clay County Juvenile Justice Center. Because the perpetrator was a juvenile, privacy laws are in effect. However, in an interview with Janet Rogers, juvenile officer for Clay County and director of Court Services, she told me that the case was adjudicated within sixty days. She stressed that their program is treatment-oriented and not punitive. It is geared to rehabilitation in order to enable the juveniles to become productive members of society. Ms. Rogers described an impressive array of programs to help those young people and their families. Among the dozen services described is "Break Free from Abuse," which includes sections on personal safety, resources, court advocate services, and impact of abuse on children. It also lists ten publications, some of which can be downloaded in Spanish as well as English. These services that can be found on the center's website include prevention, intervention, and protection for children and their families.

Extreme bullying behaviors, such as the one that occurred in Liberty, go on day in and day out all over the country in spite of bullying prevention programs that most schools now have in place. Clearly, the bully who attacked Blake had serious problems. The question we must ask is this: Why wasn't there adequate intervention to address this bully's issues before it played out in such a brutal manner? As discussed throughout this book, bullying behavior is often a call for help, and punitive action is not the answer to changing the bully's behavior. This bully and many like him require early professional intervention in order to prevent an entire life of bullying and to protect those who would be his targets. Fortunately, the Clay County Juvenile Justice Center has stepped in to provide this type of intervention for this particular bully.

Liberty, Missouri, is a suburb of Kansas City with a population of just under 30,000 and is not so different from thousands of suburbs, cities, and towns throughout the United States. What does make Liberty stand out is the immediate and overwhelming response to the incident by Liberty's citizens. Within a week, a number of these citizens attended the school board meeting to demand action to prevent a repeat of this horrific incident. They also organized a Liberty Parents Action Network on Facebook to help engage more people in the issue and keep parents informed. In addition to the community-wide action to address the problem, there was also an outpouring of support for Blake. He received over 1,200 cards and letters. His brother Andrew, a high school student, gathered 300 signatures on a petition to designate the day of Blake's attack as Bullying Awareness Day — District Wide. State representative Nick King was among those who signed the petition.

Best of all, Preston told his mother that he now thought his "fellow students were more supportive and sensitive." It can only be hoped that this will be a permanent shift in attitude among the students in the community.

ACTS OF KINDNESS

Kindness expressed after a bullying incident, like that demonstrated toward Blake and his family, can make an enormous difference in the target's life, helping that person heal, regain confidence, and feel a sense of belonging, which may have been shattered by the incident. Perhaps even better is kindness expressed to others for no particular reason at all. This category of kindness is the one that helps create an atmosphere of inclusion that may help prevent bullying from happening in the first place. The positive impact of an act of kindness could be more far-reaching than meets the eye. The recipient's mood might be lifted, and he or she may go on to perform an act of kindness toward another person. It is contagious! And these acts do not only benefit the recipient. For many people, performing an act of kindness will give them "warm fuzzies" inside that stay with them for the rest of the day.

An act of kindness can be as simple as allowing another car to enter into the flow of traffic or as profound as being an organ donor. The positive impact of an act of kindness on both parties can't be overstated.

HOW YOU CAN MAKE A DIFFERENCE

You have more power to make an impact in the prevention of bullying than you may realize.

As an individual, model kindness at all times, wherever you might be — whether it's holding the elevator door open for someone running down the hallway to catch it or listening with attention to your child.

At home keep the lines of communication open with all members of the family. It's important for you to share what you've learned about bullying with your loved ones. Be sure to apply the information you've discovered about electronic bullying and cyber bullying.

In the workplace, wherever you are in the organizational structure, help create an environment that will make it one of the "Best Places to Work" in your community. Follow the recommendations discussed in Chapter Six.

HOW YOUR COMMUNITY CAN MAKE A DIFFERENCE

Imagine taking your personal power to effect a positive change and multiplying it by ten or twenty . . . or even five hundred. That's what happens when you start sharing what you've learned about bullying prevention with a group or organization you're a part of. Organizing a "call to action" project as a group response within a major organization such as a PTA, PTO, or House of Worship gives you a cohort from which to draw. The following project drew participants from a congregational sisterhood as well as from the community at large. There are many such organizations from coast to coast.

Carol Yarmo, vice-president of Community Services of Congregation Beth Shalom in the Kansas City metropolitan area, says she was hooked when she heard one of my presentations on the topic of bullying. She took the "call to action" to heart with a passion that brought about significant results. She explains that, as a retired teacher, she "was very moved and motivated to tackle this enormous problem." She also believed she could get others in her congregation and the community interested in joining her in this effort.

Carol convened a group that became known as the Banishing Bullying Behavior (BBB) Project and provided presentations to forty-five groups in the first year alone, reaching 727 individuals from early childhood to senior adulthood.

Experts in the field of bullying behavior generally agree that one-time annual anti-bullying programs, no matter how effective, are not enough to assure a bully-free environment within a school. The Liberty Middle School bully attack is a classic example of a school district that has one or two large anti-bullying programs without periodic follow-up programs. One of the goals of the BBB Project is to provide smaller, ongoing anti-bullying programs in the schools, the workplace, and retirement facilities to fill in the gaps and help create bully-free environments. As the BBB Project has gained community visibility, social agencies such as Boys and Girls Clubs, CASA, Scouts, and so on, began to call on us to work with their students and volunteers, as well.

Andrew Bash, our Chapter Three bully, has been affectionately called a "rock star" by the students he works with each year at St. Therese School in Parkville, Missouri. He works with the upper-grade students while Joan Jacobson, Robbie Bossert, and Ellen Rothman work with the lower elementary school students. Their outstanding presentations in classrooms reinforce the major anti-bullying school-wide program by a national expert at the beginning of each school year. This format has proven to be the most effective, and a visitor to St. Therese School can feel the environment of happy students.

One of the most effective programs Andrew has conducted was for over 300 high school freshmen — sharing his journey. For almost an hour you could hear a pin drop, and afterwards some students were inspired to make amends even in such a large group. Andrew has been invited to make his presentation in other high schools as well.

Another member of our group, a school psychologist, has moved to California and wants to continue to work there as a member of our group. He was actually asked by a group of sixth-grade students to conduct some sessions for them.

My presentations as a member of the BBB Project include senior citizen church groups, college and university pre-service teachers, and workplace settings.

You'll find detailed guidelines of how to organize and implement a program such as the BBB Project in the Appendix at the end of this book.

HOW PEERS CAN MAKE A DIFFERENCE

There is nothing more impactful than hearing someone's personal story. It takes courage to stand up in front of a crowded room and tell your experience with bullying — whichever side of the equation you were on. This is exactly what took place in Andrew Rossbach's fourth-grade classroom, and it was his older sister Kristen who made it happen. Kristen Rossbach was a student in the tenth grade at Darien High School in Darien, Connecticut, when she initiated a program in response to her younger brother being targeted. She felt so sorry for him as he relayed the daily episodes of typical bullying behavior that she decided to put together a panel of her peers. The panel consisted of two boys and two girls who spoke to Andrew's class about their experiences with bullying. One of the boys spoke about his experience as a bully; the other boy talked about having been a bystander instead of a witness. One of the girls told how she had overcome having been the victim of "mean girls" in middle school, and Kristen demonstrated anti-bullying exercises she had learned when she was in third grade.

"I'm twenty-five years old now," Kristen said, "and I still remember the graphic exercises my third-grade teacher demonstrated for our class to illustrate the devastating effect bullying can have on the bully's victim. The boys in Andrew's class were especially impressed by the popular high school boys who were macho athletes and spoke to them that day. The panel had a very positive effect on the class." Kristen's story underscores the very positive lasting effect anti-bullying education can have.

Another program, called Be a Buddy — Not a Bully, was started by fourth grader Isabella Griffin in Alamosa, Colorado. The year before she developed the program, she had been bullied by a group of mean girls for her clothing and for not having the most recent electronics. Later, witnessing a special-needs student become the victim of bullying was the tipping point for her, and she decided to act, with the help of her dad and the support of her school administration. Thus, was launched Be a Buddy — Not a Bully. Today the program has an extensive website, opportunities for students to volunteer in a number of anti-bullying programs, events, projects, and a "Bully Pledge:"

Say it loud and be proud!!!

I will be respectful to myself and others. I will be a friend to those who are being bullied. I will stand up! And step in! And I will be a buddy and not a bully.

Many schools have similar pledges, some written by students, others suggested by guest speakers or bullying prevention programs. The Tyler Clementi Upstander Pledge is an excellent example of a pledge that addresses many bullying issues and suggests actions you can take to respond to them. Read the following pledge carefully; it has much to teach us about choosing the role of witness (or, in the language of the pledge, Upstander) rather than simply being a bystander.

THE UPSTANDER PLEDGE

- I pledge to become an Upstander by standing up to bullying whether I'm at school, at home, at work, in my house of worship, or out with friends, family, colleagues, or teammates.
- I will work to make others feel safe and included by treating them with respect and compassion.
- I will not use insulting or demeaning language, slurs, gestures, facial expressions, or jokes about anyone's sexuality, size, gender, race, any kind of disability, religion, class, politics, or other differences in person or while using technology.
- I will state my disagreement or discomfort about people's differences in ways that are respectful rather than insulting or demeaning.
- I will encourage my peers, family members, and colleagues to do the same and will speak up when they use prejudiced language about any group for any reason.

If I see or hear behavior that perpetuates prejudice occurring:

- I will speak up! I will let others know that bullying, cruelty, and prejudice are abusive and not acceptable.
- I will reach out to someone I know who has been the target of abusive actions or words and let this person know that this is not okay with me and ask how I can help.
- I will remain vigilant and not be a passive audience or "bystander" to abusive actions or words.
- I will reach out to someone I think might be suffering from abusive actions by others to offer my support and make it a point to spend time with this person.

- I will tell everyone who is in a position of authority in this group, such as a teacher, coach, caregiver, manager, or religious leader, about what I saw and heard and make sure there is follow-up.
- I will seek help from trusted friends, colleagues, professionals, and other resources if I don't know what to do or need support to take action.

If I learn in person or online that someone is feeling very depressed or potentially suicidal:
- I will reach out and tell this person, "Your life has value and is important, no matter how you feel at the moment and no matter what others say or think."
- I will strongly encourage this person to get professional help.
- I will get professional help about what to do myself if I am worried that someone might be considering suicide.

If you'd like to sign this pledge or print it out, you can do so at the Tyler Clementi Foundation's website: www.tylerclementi.org. A careful reading of the pledge provides an excellent understanding of what we can and should do in response to the call to action. Too many tragic deaths have occurred since the *Sioux City Journal* editorial "call to action."

When I conducted the very first interview for this book, I never thought that the Commander-in-Chief in the most important workplace on earth would earn the title of Bully-in-Chief! This has had a ripple effect across the nation and worldwide.

Some educators report that the progress made by anti-bullying programs required in schools has continued to be effective while others have noted some rise in bullying behavior. This made our work to banish bullying behavior all the more important.

It is my hope that, as you continue to think about the people you have met in this book, you will respond to the call to action as an individual and as a member of a kinder, gentler society.

"OUR OPINION: WE MUST STOP BULLYING. IT STARTS HERE. IT STARTS NOW." *SIOUX CITY JOURNAL* EDITORIAL BOARD, APRIL 22, 2012

Siouxland lost a young life to a senseless, shameful tragedy last week. By all accounts, Kenneth Weishuhn was a kind-hearted, fun-loving teenage boy, always looking to make others smile. But when the South O'Brien High School fourteen-year-old told friends he was gay — the harassment and bullying began. It didn't let up until he took his own life.

Sadly, Kenneth's story is far from unique. Boys and girls across Iowa and beyond are targeted every day. In this case sexual orientation appears to have played a role, but we have learned a bully needs no reason to strike. No sense can be made of these actions.

Now our community and region must face this stark reality: We are all to blame. We have not done enough. Not nearly enough.

This is not a failure of one group of kids, one school, one town, one county, or one geographic area. Rather, it exposes a fundamental flaw in our society, one that has deep-seated roots. Until now, it has been too difficult, inconvenient — maybe even painful — to address. But we can't keep looking away.

In Kenneth's case, the warnings were everywhere. We saw it happen in other communities; now it has hit home. Undoubtedly, it wasn't the first life lost to bullying here, but we can strive to make it the last.

The documentary "Bully," which depicts the bullying of an East Middle School student, opened in Sioux City on Friday. We urge everyone to see it. At its core, it is a heartbreaking tale of how far we have yet to go. Despite its award-winning, proactive policies, we see there is still much work to be done in Sioux City schools.

Superintendent Paul Gausman is absolutely correct when he says, "it takes all of us to solve the problem." But schools must be at the forefront of our battle against bullying.

Sioux City must continue to strengthen its resolve and its policies. Clearly, South O'Brien High School needs to alter its approach. We urge Superintendent Dan Moore to rethink his stance that "we have all the things in place to deal with it." It should be evident that is simply not the case.

South O'Brien isn't the only school that needs help. A *Journal Des*

Moines bureau report last year demonstrated that too many schools don't take bullying seriously. According to that report, Iowa school districts, on average, reported less than two percent of their students had been bullied in any given year since the state passed its anti-bullying law in 2007. That statistic belies the actual depth of this problem, and in response the Iowa Department of Education will implement a more comprehensive anti-bullying and harassment policy in the 2012-13 school year.

But as Gausman and Nate Monson, director of Iowa Safe Schools, are quick to remind us, this is more than a school problem. If we want to eradicate bullying in our community, we can't rely on schools alone.

We need to support local agencies like the Waitt Institute for Violence Prevention and national efforts like the one described at www.stopbullying.gov. Bullying takes many forms, some of them — Internet, Facebook, cell phone — more subtle than others. Parents should monitor the cell phone and Internet usage of their children. All public and private institutions need to do more to demonstrate that bullying is simply unacceptable in our workplaces and in our homes. We need to educate ourselves and others.

Some in our community will say bullying is simply a part of life. If no one is physically hurt, they will say, what's the big deal? It's just boys being boys and girls being girls.

Those people are wrong, and they must be shouted down.

We must make it clear in our actions and our words that bullying will not be tolerated. Those of us in public life must be ever mindful of the words we choose, especially in the contentious political debates that have defined our modern times. More importantly, we must not be afraid to act.

How many times has each of us witnessed an act of bullying and said little or nothing? After all, it wasn't our responsibility. A teacher or an official of some kind should step in. If our kid wasn't involved, we figured, it's none of our business.

- Try to imagine explaining that rationale to the mother of Kenneth Weishuhn.
- It is the business of all of us. More specifically, it is our responsibility. Our mandate.
- If we're honest with ourselves, we will acknowledge our community

has yet to view bullying in quite this way. It's well past time to do so.
- Stand up. Be heard. And don't back down. Together, we can put a stop to bullying.

APPENDIX

PREPARATION FOR ACTION

As vice-President for Social Action, Carol has a list of about fifty volunteers whom she thought might be interested in volunteering to participate in the Banishing Bullying Behavior Project. She called everyone on her list personally, as well as anyone else who would listen! Carol invited them to one of two meetings, one in the morning and the second set for late afternoon, to accommodate work schedules.

Carol and I prepared a packet of information, including the *Sioux City Journal* editorial article, for everyone who attended. We also prepared an agenda that gave attendees background information and an opportunity to brainstorm about how to organize as a group. About thirty-five people attended, expressed a great deal of interest but also wanted more information before they were ready to commit to participate in the project. We did explain that there were opportunities to participate without doing presentations or leading discussion groups. Outreach, publicity, and research are all areas that can be considered "behind the scenes" participation — perfect for those who might not feel comfortable speaking to groups of people.

Interested participants were asked to read *Banishing Bullying Behavior: Transforming the Culture of Peer Abuse*, which would serve as the text and the basis for presentations. About a month later we convened a second meeting, again with two time options, that was attended by about forty-five people. SuEllen Fried, co-author of my first two books, and I both brainstormed with the group to envision ways they might take the message to audiences of all ages.

Several training sessions followed to give participants the confidence to make presentations. I provided the group with an outline based on our book that I use for my own presentations, urging each person to adapt the outline to his or her public speaking style.

From training sessions, we moved to monthly workshops, at which participants started practicing their presentations and we played the audience, be it preschool students, kindergarten through second grade, third through fifth grade, middle and high school students, adult audiences, senior citizen residents, and college and university student teachers. Our group includes retired teachers and counselors, docents, businessmen and women, as well "professional volunteers" and those still active in the field of education, business, or other professions. Following each presentation, the group discussed the high points and made suggestions for changes that might strengthen the presentation.

Carol spent a tremendous amount of time and energy meeting with individuals to promote our presentations. This included chairs of Departments of Education, leaders of youth groups and Boy Scouts, school administrators, and classroom teachers, just to mention a few. We reached groups spanning a wide range of ages — from preschool children to senior adults living in retirement homes. As discussed in Chapter Ten we found our work in this area to be very much appreciated.

Without going into all the details, suffice it to say that I think the format established by the BBB Project can readily be replicated in many different settings. Carol Yarmo's passion about the need to respond to the call for action was a major factor in the success of the BBB Project. For her it was a twenty-four/seven commitment. So, the first step is to find a person or persons for whom the call to action requires an immediate response.

PLANNING AND BRAINSTORMING

Organizing as an offshoot of an established organization such as the PTA, a PTO, a sisterhood, or a church auxiliary gives the "call to action" a base from which to draw. A small steering committee should make personal calls to explain the purpose of the project and to invite prospective participants to attend an organizational meeting. We found having two meetings, each at a different time of day, a very effective approach for reaching a diverse group of people.

Once the time and place have been established, an agenda for the meeting should be drawn up and informational packets prepared. The packets should include the *Sioux City Journal* editorial board call to action article, a generic outline for presentations, opportunities for participation, a copy of the Table of Contents of *Banishing Bullying Behavior: Transforming the Culture of Peer Abuse,* and plenty of paper for note taking.

Following is a copy of the agenda that was followed at the

organizational meeting and proved to be very effective. It can be adapted to your individual organization.

ORGANIZATIONAL MEETING

Agenda
1. Welcome
2. Introductions
   a. Steering Committee
   b. Participants introduce themselves with one or two sentences about their interest in being able to respond to the call to action
3. Convener of the meeting presents background of the call to action and various opportunities for participation.
4. Open the floor for questions and discussion
5. Announce time and place for next meeting
6. Good and welfare

OPPORTUNITIES FOR PARTICIPATION

As mentioned earlier, there are many opportunities to participate in a BBB Project, both as presenters and discussion leaders as well as behind the scenes. The following is a description of the various tasks participants can choose to participate in:

Presenters/discussion leaders: Prepare and make presentations to "book groups," church and synagogue organizations, youth groups and Scouts, senior citizens, PTA and PTO, and schools of education that prepare teachers at colleges and universities. The presentation should be followed by question-and-answer session. and a discussion of the material covered during the presentation.

Outreach: Contact individuals representing the aforementioned groups and arrange to meet with them to explain the importance of ongoing anti-bullying education and how your presentations will enrich and support the work they are already doing. Prepare a list of personal contacts whom you think might be interested in having your BBB Project present for their school or group.

PowerPoint presentations: Individuals who are interested in making

PowerPoint presentations and/or would like to learn to make these presentations can use their expertise in this area to enhance presentations.

"Book Ladies": Work with librarians, media specialists, and classroom teachers to arrange a time to read a book that teaches an anti-bullying lesson to a class during their library day period or in the classroom. Facilitate a discussion following the reading. "Book Ladies" might also conduct "Book Chats" for students during their lunch hour. Suggested format for discussions is the Junior Great Books open-ended questions.

Discussion leader: Follow up sessions in the classrooms that have state-mandated anti-bullying programs. These programs can be very effective, but research indicates one or two programs a year are not sufficient. There should be follow-up discussions on an ongoing basis.

Researcher: Develop a list of appropriate books for children's anti-bullying literature and class discussions based on grade levels. Conduct ongoing online research presenting the most current information for speakers and discussion leaders. Ascertain how school districts and individual schools are implementing state-mandated anti-bullying programs to enable speakers and discussion leaders to reinforce these programs.

Develop a library of books on bullying as a resource for participants in the BBB Project.

Adult advocates: One of the major problems that needs to be addressed in order to banish bullying behavior is *"hot spots":* school buses, hallways, lunchrooms, playgrounds, and restrooms. For example, bus drivers tell us that they report bullying on their buses to their respective administrations, and yet "the administrators don't do anything about it." We can become advocates to see that this changes. In the documentary movie "Bully," one of the mothers pleads for intervention by saying, "When I rode the school bus if anyone misbehaved, they were no longer permitted to ride the bus. Why can't that be enforced today?"

Adult advocates can be very helpful to do just that — advocate for the need to intervene when bullying occurs.

OUTREACH AND NETWORKING

Recruit individuals who recognize the urgent need to "sell a program" that will educate the public — of all ages — to do what is necessary to combat bullying behavior and turn the tide of what has become a problem of epidemic proportions.

Reach out to all segments of the community; you can do this through networking opportunities from early childhood through senior adulthood. This should be followed by compiling a list to make phone calls in order to set up appointments with a contact person for the organizations and academic institutions. At each appointment, discuss and outline the BBB Project, its mission, and the system you will use to deliver it. Hopefully, by the end of the visit the contact person will be convinced of the importance of having supplemental programs on an ongoing basis for their students or clientele. It is important to set a date for your group to make a presentation.

TRAINING SESSIONS

Once the participants have read the Fried/Sosland text, one or two training sessions should be sufficient to prepare them to make presentations. Participants in BBB programs have found it very helpful to have a generic outline of the material they'll be covering during presentations.

As mentioned earlier, we became the "audience" for each presenter and were able to learn from one another. We role-played the age of the grade level of the students, adults, or senior adults. The participants found the training sessions to be tremendous confidence builders. Although many in the group are retired teachers, they expressed the need to "get comfortable" with the subject matter.

PRESENTATIONS

During the first couple of years presentations were made to preschool classes, early elementary grades, upper elementary students, middle school and high school, student teachers, adults, and senior adults. BBB project participants reported on their presentations to the group at our regular meetings. This was and is another opportunity to learn from one another.

PLANNING AHEAD

The Sisterhood BBB Project participants continue to work with student teachers as well as with the schools and organizations described in the Appendix. They are also trained to address the issues of workplace bullying and to prepare presentations to help business and professional organizations create healthy workplace environments.

EARLY CHILDHOOD PRESENTATION

In 2009 when I began to research bullying behavior there was virtually no bullying in early childhood settings. There might have been some "bossiness" that prompt intervention prevented from becoming bullying. Now ten years later the widespread lack of civility at-large has found its way to early childhood classrooms.

Our BBB Project has responded to requests for presentations for early childhood teachers. Following is the outline for such a presentation by Joan Jacobson, who has a MS in guidance and counseling and has had a distinguished career in advanced education counseling. This model presentation can be adapted for presentations at all age levels.

PREVENTING BULLYING IN EARLY CHILDHOOD SETTINGS

As educators, we know that we have a lasting impact in the lives of the children we work with. Although there are other factors in these children's lives that contribute to their behavior, what happens in the classroom has a powerful effect. Although you are already responsible for so much — educating, communicating, soothing ruffled feathers of parents as well as children, there are things you can do in the preschool setting to prevent, stop, and change bullying behaviors. We can teach children who bully **SOCIAL SKILLS** to interact in positive ways; we can help children who are targets **DEVELOP STRATEGIES** to become resilient against bullying, and we can show witnesses ways to **SUPPORT** a child who is a target that counteract the hurt and make themselves feel good.

Let's talk about how early bullying behaviors develop, and then I'll provide activities and exercises that you can do with your children to be more intentional in making this happen.

HOW DOES EARLY BULLYING DEVELOP?

Young children bring with them a history of experiences with **FAMILY**, media, or other children. Physical punishment or use of physical or verbal aggression to control others, may lead children to initiate aggressive behaviors.

In early childhood settings bullying is often overlooked ... kids too naïve and innocent; "kids will be kids;" some kids just challenging; can't see everything in class.

Young children (two to four years old) may observe others using aggressive behaviors to defend their possessions. Older children (four to six years old) may threaten or intimidate.

If not stopped, young children who bully will continue to bully, and children who are victimized will continue to be targets.

Early bullying may lead to abusive teen dating relationships, domestic violence, or other criminal activities.

PRE-BULLYING BEHAVIORS LEAD TO BULLYING

Young children experiment with different ways of behaving that may be precursors to bullying ... may ***turn into a pattern*** of bullying.
- **MAIN DETERMINER (RESPONSE OF THE TARGET):** Cries, submits, yields the toy — likely to target the same child again.
- **CONTAGIOUS:** "Successful" display of power and dominance; others may join in. **HIERARCHIES** develop over several months.
- **GENDER-SPECIFIC BEHAVIORS: Boys:** direct physical/verbal; **Girls:** more subtle; **Relational:** exclusion, secrets, threaten not to play — more difficult to detect.

PARTICULAR BEHAVIORS TO PAY ATTENTION TO:
- Shouting "mine" while grabbing a toy.
- Whispering secrets and calling each other silly names.
- "You can't play with me."
- Make-believe ... child who consistently takes charge and assigns one child less desirable role.

BULLIES, VICTIMS, BYSTANDERS

COMMON COMPONENTS OF BULLYING:
- **DELIBERATE:** A bully's intention is to hurt someone.
- **REPEATED:** Often targets the same victim.
- **POWER IMBALANCE:** Target seen as vulnerable.
- **PHYSICAL:** Hitting, shoving, pinching, throwing objects, taking toy, ruining art.

- **VERBAL:** Calling names, threatening to take a toy away, telling secrets.
- **RELATIONAL:** Ignoring, excluding, whispering, "You can't play with us." Running away, encouraging others to join in, isolating.

A child who bullies identifies a vulnerable child to target (lacks friends or responds with *passive acceptance* or *uncontrolled outbursts*). They know how to hide their behavior from adults or blame target.

INTERVENTION:

To prevent continuing and escalating bullying let children know that it is ***not allowed*** and ***will not be tolerated.***

TARGETS — NEED TO LOOK OUT FOR MOST AT RISK:
- Small, weak, insecure, sensitive, or "different" from their peers.
- Often shy, have difficulty making friends, prefer to play alone.
- Submissive, lack the assertiveness to say, "No" or "Stop that."
- Children who get excluded from social groups or are targets of other children's hurtful behaviors.

Once children become repeated targets of bullying, other children often show a dislike for them. Children avoid or exclude victimized children because they want to maintain their position in the ***social hierarchy*** and fear becoming targets themselves. Targets become withdrawn, isolated, and reluctant to join social groups.
- Physical symptoms, sad, depressed, and may refuse to go to school.
- Need to know that adults care about their situation and can help.
- Need guidance to respond assertively and effectively.

WITNESSES — all who observe the behaviors (Upstanders):
- May not know what to do to help.
- May do nothing out of fear they will be next.
- May have become desensitized based on their experiences in home or media.

CONSEQUENCES:
- May feel **GUILTY** later or **JOIN IN** — at risk for becoming bullies themselves.

- **NEED TO UNDERSTAND THAT THEY HAVE THE POWER TO STOP** the bullying.
- **NEED HELP IN DEVELOPING AND PRACTICING THE PROBLEM-SOLVING AND ASSERTIVENESS SKILLS TO STAND UP FOR THEIR PEERS AND FEEL SAFE** — will make them feel proud for helping another child.

WHAT WE CAN DO:
- Children who bully need to learn to engage in more cooperative behaviors and develop **EMPATHY.**
- Children who are targets need to learn how to respond with **ASSERTIVENESS** rather than by submitting or counter-attacking.
- Bystanders need to learn that they have the power to stop bullying and use **PROBLEM-SOLVING STRATEGIES** to help prevent and stop bullying.

TALK about bullying. Dealing directly and openly lets them know that:
- Bullying is an important concern.
- It will **NOT** be tolerated.
- Everyone needs to work together to stop and prevent.

Children who understand what bullying is and the forms it takes are better able to recognize it. If they understand that it hurts and why it's not permitted, they are more likely to respond appropriately and ask for help.

HELP CHILDREN UNDERSTAND THE THREE CHARACTERISTICS OF BULLYING:
- It's on purpose.
- It happens over and over again.
- It involves the abuse of power to hurt others.

HELP CHILDREN UNDERSTAND THE THREE WAYS BULLYING CAN HAPPEN:
- **VERBAL:** Using words to hurt.
- **PHYSICAL:** Using actions to hurt.
- **RELATIONAL:** Using friendships to hurt (excluding people, saying someone can't be your friend, turning someone's friends against that person, rumors.)

GROUP MEETINGS:

In morning meetings or circle time, ensure that everyone knows the **EXPECTATIONS**. Engage all in setting classroom rules, identifying and solving bullying problems, becoming helpful bystanders, engaging in acts of kindness, and **MAKING SURE THAT ALL CHILDREN FEEL SAFE AND INCLUDED**.

ACTIVITIES FOR TALKING ABOUT BULLYING:

If children are reluctant to talk about bullying start by sharing a story about when you were bullied or witnessed bullying. Ask them to share some stories about bullying that happened outside the classroom that did not involve their own classmates. Ask them not to use real names.

TEASING/TAUNTING (TEASING THAT HURTS). GIVE EXAMPLES:
- Scott runs very fast: "Rocket Scott."
- Jeremy is always last in a race: "Snaily Jerry."
- Maria is strong: "Wonder girl."
- Steve is small and cries a lot: "Baby Steve."

ASK:
- "How can you tell if a name is playful or hurtful?"
- Intent: Is the name-caller trying to be nice or mean?
- How do you think the child with the nickname feels?

ACCIDENT OR ON PURPOSE:
- Jake steps on Ray's toe by accident and says, "I'm sorry."
- Tony is mad at Robert and stomps hard on his toe.
- Emily doesn't see Eddie's tower of blocks and knocks it over.
- Beth doesn't like Christine, so she scribbles all over her picture.

"YOU CAN'T SAY YOU CAN'T PLAY:"
Intentionally and repeatedly excluding certain children from play groups is **UNACCEPTABLE**.
- Have children brainstorm ways they might respond when this happens.
- Ask if you can play in a little while, etc. **ROLE-PLAY** different responses.
- Brainstorm things a bystander could say to help the child being excluded.

Reading books out loud to children about bullying provides opportunities to talk about how other children experience and respond to bullying. Follow up with questions.

ACTIVITIES TO DEVELOP THE SOCIAL SKILLS THEY NEED TO PREVENT BULLYING

EMPATHY .... ASSERTIVENESS .... PROBLEM SOLVING

Children who can **EMPATHIZE** respond caringly to what others think and feel. They understand that bullying hurts. They are less likely to bully and more likely to help children who are bullied.

Children who are **ASSERTIVE** can stand up for themselves and others and are less likely to be targets.

Educators can help young children use a variety of constructive, non-aggressive **PROBLEM-SOLVING** skills to help stop and prevent bullying.

ACTIVITIES FOR TEACHING EMPATHY SKILLS

1. **Labeling feelings:** Ask children to describe how they might feel in three bullying situations:
   - If they saw someone being bullied;
   - If they were being bullied;
   - If they bullied someone.

Explain that bullying can lead to strong feelings — anger, frustration, fear. It's okay to feel these feelings, not okay to react by intentionally hurting someone. If we all work together, no one will ever need to experience these feelings as a result of bullying.

2. **Different and similar:** Discuss the ways that children are different from each other: big/small, run fast/slow, some like Legos/others draw. "What would it be like if we were all the same?" (Boring). *The differences make us stronger, more interesting, better able to do different things.*

Ways they are similar: eat, sleep, grow, have feelings, **HURT** when bullied. No one likes to be bullied. Never bully someone because he or she is **DIFFERENT**.

3. **Helping others feel better:** Ask children …
   - "How can you know how someone else feels*?" Listen, ask, look at face and body.*
   - "How can we recognize when another child is feeling bad or left out?"
   - "How can we cheer up children who feel bad and help them feel better? *Pay attention to them, pat on back, ask them to play with you.*

   Use **ROLE-PLAY** to help children practice recognizing a child who is feeling hurt and helping the child feel better. Divide into pairs, switching roles of bully/bystander.

4. **Acts of kindness:** Opposite of bullying.
   - Ask children to describe one nice thing they did for someone. *How did it make the other person/them feel?*
   - Plan one act of kindness they will do that day and report.

5. "**The Golden Rule**": "Do to others as you would want them to do to you." *Ask for examples of things they don't want done to them/would like done.*

6. **Helpfulness:** Use pictures, stories, or puppets to model examples

ASSERTIVENESS ACTIVITIES — ROLE-PLAY

Learn how to respond in bullying situations by standing up for themselves and others in non-aggressive and respectful ways. Learning how to express one's own feelings and defending one's rights while respecting feelings and rights of others. Learn **ASSERTIVENESS SKILLS** as an alternative to aggressive behavior in boys and submissive behaviors in girls.

1. **Keeping cool:** Simple relaxation and self-calming techniques.
Discuss how they may feel in a bullying situation — angry, fearful, sad, upset, embarrassed, confused. What do you want to do? — yell, throw something, hit, hide, cry, make another person feel bad? *Are these good or helpful?*

Ask to describe and demonstrate things to keep calm and cool-headed (Have the group choose best. Practice using them.):
- Close eyes and take several slow deep breaths.
- Count to ten.
- Stand tall.
- Relax the muscles in your face and body.
- Silently repeat a soothing phrase, "Keep calm" or "I control my feelings."
- Get a drink of water.
- Sit by a person you trust.

2. **Ignoring:** Child who bullies often seeking a reaction.
- Ignore (bully may lose interest).
- Stop playing/walk away/turn body away/don't answer.

3. **"Yes" or "No":** It's okay to refuse a bully's demand: "Give me that!" But when asked politely one can choose.

4. **Standing up to bullying:** Of self or others gives a sense of **CONTROL**, air of **SELF-CONFIDENCE** that can deter others from bullying them.

STAND UP ...... SPEAK UP...... ASK AN ADULT FOR HELP

PROBLEM-SOLVING ACTIVITIES — PRACTICE HELPS YOUNG CHILDREN TO USE SKILLS

1. WHAT IF?
- **Physical bullying:** Boy pushes other off bench; friends laugh, target cries.
- **Verbal bullying:** After visiting zoo, girl calls another "hippo."
- **Relational bullying:** Girl tells others not to play with child — now all say, "too busy."

Ask children to think of several responses — choose the best. Teacher plays bully, children take turns playing target and bystanders.

RULES ABOUT BULLYING APPROPRIATE FOR EARLY CHILDHOOD SETTING
- Bullying is not allowed.
- Stand up for yourself and your friends.
- Don't fight back.
- It's okay to walk away or ask for help.
- Include everyone in your play and activities. "You can't say, 'you can't play.'"
- Report bullying — telling is not tattling.

IMMEDIATE INTERVENTION
- Teachers need to immediately stop the bullying by saying "**STOP**" and paying minimal attention to the child who is bullying.
- State the "No bullying" rule.
- Briefly describe the behavior you observed and why it is not allowed.
- **TALK** to the child bully separately at a later time.
- **COACH** the target to respond assertively
- **ENGAGE** bystanders to support the child being bullied.

LISTEN AND VALIDATE FEELINGS/ASK FOR DETAILS/
SAY YOU CAN HELP/TALK ABOUT SOLUTIONS

Children who bully must understand that bullying is not acceptable and will not be allowed.

Children who are targets must know that adults care and support them, that they ***do not deserve to be bullied***, and that they can ask adults and peers to help them. They need help and practice responding assertively to bullying.

Children who are bystanders must understand that they have the power to intervene — asking bully to stop, helping target walk away, asking for adult help.

MODEL PRESCHOOL PRESENTATION
BY ROBBIE BOSSERT AND ELLEN ROTHMAN

I. Good morning boys and girls. My name is Miss Robbie and this is Ms. Ellen. We are from a group called Banishing Bullying Behavior, which is part of Beth Shalom Sisterhood.

II. We want to talk to you about **KINDNESS**, **EMPATHY**, and **DIVERSITY** in your classroom, and on the playground. Also, we would like you to share any stories or questions after we read some books about getting along.

III. **Robbie:** Introduces *One* ... one of my favorite books.
    A. Discussion: What is an **UPSTANDER**? Number one is an upstander. He or she is a bystander who stands up for the person being bullied. They are very important people.
    B. I will give your teachers a number one for each of you to color.

IV. **Ellen:** What is **EMPATHY**? (Robbie holds up a sign.)
    A. It is the ability to share someone's feelings. It is like the expression, "to walk in someone else's shoes."
    B. I'm going to read a portion of the book about empathy.
    C. Read the book. Take questions and listen to personal stories.

V. The **GOLDEN RULE**. (Robbie Holds up sign.)
  A. Talk about the golden rule and how it is important no matter how old you are.
  B. Discuss.

VI. **DIVERSITY.**
  A. Robbie reads part of the book, *Unique*.
  B. Discuss.

VII. Read *Beautiful Hands* by Kathryn Otoshi.
  A. Discuss.

VIII. Teach hand gestures.
  A. Walk away
  B. Tell someone safe like a teacher, parent, etc.
  C. Buddy up

VIIII. Thank you for inviting us to your class and letting us share these books and thoughts with you and your teacher.

X. Pass out stickers.

"What has been will be again, what has been done will be done again; there is nothing new under the sun."
— **Ecclesiastes 1:19**

Bullying goes back to Biblical days. All one has to do is Google "bullying in the Bible" and one finds many Biblical sources. Although there is nothing new about the concept of bullying it has taken on many new forms. We do have many new resources and much research to help us in our work to banish bullying behavior. I hope this model and information will encourage you to find a way to respond to the call for action.

If you have any questions or would like additional information, please feel free to contact me by email: blanche@soslandphoto.com.

ACKNOWLEDGEMENTS

My first two books, *Banishing Bullying Behavior: Transforming the Culture of Pain, Rage and Revenge* and *Banishing Bullying Behavior: Transforming the Culture of Peer Abuse*, were co-authored with SuEllen Fried as textbooks for undergraduate and graduate students of teacher education. Much to my surprise the books were read by a number of prominent business leaders and authors around the country. Morton Sosland, retired editor-in-chief of Sosland Publishing Company, was the first to send me a note after reading our first book, "You must write a book for the business world." It was followed by a conversation with Jerry Goodman, well known as an American author, also known by pseudonym Adam Smith, an economics broadcast commentator, and as George Goodman, author of fiction, who had the same message for me. Kurt Mayer, Tacoma businessman and author of *My Personal Brush with History*, also urged me to write this book. However, it was a doctoral student, who asked not to be identified, and who jumped out of her seat during a guest lecture I presented to her class at the University of Kansas, and said emphatically, "You MUST write this book about bullying in the business world." I am most grateful to all four individuals for their understanding of the need for this book.

My sincere appreciation to the honorable Howard F. Sachs for introducing me to the study of epigenetics and for making the connection of the relevance with my work on this book. We are all the beneficiaries of his wisdom and insight.

To Nomi Isak go my sincere thanks for sharing her tremendous talent as an editor and writing coach. All my previous writing had been academics so to author a book for the general public required a tremendous amount of coaching on the part of this outstanding editor of my first manuscript.

Most of the individuals acknowledged in our first edition of *Banishing Bullying Behavior* continued to make meaningful contributions as I worked on this new book, especially Nancy Mailman who sent countless articles clipped from newspapers and magazines from all over the country.

It is difficult to find words adequate to express my appreciation to Jane Clementi for taking the time to read my manuscript and sharing her wisdom and insight with me and the readers of my book in her foreword. My admiration for her ability to turn her family's tragedy into a powerful program to save others from the pain and loss she has experienced knows no limits. May Tyler's memory always be for a blessing.

I have long admired Marc Solomon's work as an author, most notably, *Winning Marriage: The Inside Story of How Same-Sex Couples Took on the Politicians and Pundits — and Won.* His work has been published in the *Boston Globe, Huffington Post, Advocate,* among many others. I was truly honored when he offered to read my manuscript and write the very meaningful introduction for my book.

Dr. Gustave Eisemann, affectionately known as Dr. Gus, is a highly respected and beloved physician who practiced medicine for over fifty years. I am most grateful for the many hours he spent with me sharing his knowledge of bullying in the field of medicine from medical school through senior adulthood. Although we are cousins, he is more like the brother I always wished to have.

The fact that an individual of the stature of the honorable Howard A. Levine was interested in my work about bullying was inspiring and energizing for me. I am most grateful for the wealth of knowledge and experience he shared with me and in turn the readers of this book.

Steven Prince knows more about bullying in more workplace venues than anyone I have ever met. He took time from a very busy schedule for long-distance conference calls to share his tremendous knowledge to benefit the readers of this book. For this I am most grateful.

Ruth Eisemann Fost, sister, best friend and colleague all wrapped into one. Collaborating on banishing bullying behavior for Pushcart Players was very special as are all our life-long shared experiences.

My warmest appreciation to Janet Milone for the many hours she worked on the edited versions of these chapters.

To Susannah Goodman, who took time during an all-too-short family vacation to edit a chapter that desperately needed a fresh eye, goes my heartfelt appreciation.

To dear friend and colleague Nancy Somers, thank you for sharing your enormous talent with so many members of our family and for sending the "call to action" opinion piece from Sioux City via Cambridge to me in Kansas City.

I am so grateful for the time Theresa M. Barbo shared with me given her very busy schedule writing and speaking. We are so fortunate to be the beneficiaries of her enormous talent as an author, historian, and lecturer.

Dr. Joy Koesten has been a long-time colleague and friend, and her contributions to this book were made both as a colleague and friend with many shared interests.

In addition to her many professional commitments Dr. Koesten has made tremendous contributions to the state of Kansas as a member of the legislature. I know I speak on behalf of your many supporters when I say, "Thank you, Joy, for all you have accomplished."

One would never know from the ambitious schedule he keeps that Dr. Don Breckon is retired. I am so grateful that he was able to take the time to read this manuscript. His leadership and friendship at Park University provided a bully-free work environment that prompted Dr. Dale Lauritzen to say, "Let's not tell them how much we enjoy our jobs, or they'll stop paying us!"

To Dr. Deborah Sosland-Edelman, Alan Edelman, Dr. Jane and Josh Sosland, Abby Sosland, Mark Goodman, Dr. Jeffrey Sosland, Mindy Sosland, Dr. Rachel and David Sosland, our children and children by marriage, my heartfelt thanks for your ongoing vigilance and sharing of the latest research in the field of bullying. Your role modeling as parents and acts of kindness are an inspiration to me and so many others.

Special thanks go to Josh Sosland, outstanding journalist and editor, who devoted many, many hours to editing these chapters. Often, just changing a word or phrase made all the difference and left me wondering why I hadn't written it that way in the first place! It is Josh's ability to find just the right word or phrase that has enhanced the quality of this book. I am most grateful for his professional guidance and encouragement throughout the creative process.

My gratitude goes to David Sosland for always being there to help with technical tasks and challenges. In addition, his proof reading was a tremendous help in the final stages of this manuscript. And last, but far from least, he finally ended up with the huge task of publisher! This was a task that took an enormous amount of patience with the author who kept remembering "one more thing that had to be added to the manuscript."

"You should never judge a book by its cover," is an old admonition yet many people do just that. So, the selection of a cover is very important. Rachel Pase Sosland, M.D., is the personification of what is best in the field of medicine. Yet she took time from her very busy professional schedule and family time to help with this key choice in the production of this book.

To our next generation, Alex, Katja, Ari, Jonathan, Sam, Max, Leah, Zachary, Kate, Henry, Sophie, Lily, Ethan, Gabs, Jake, and Juliet, your extraordinary accomplishments at your young ages are an inspiration to all who know you. May you continue to go from strength to strength. And to Noa Dorit, you have accomplished what I never dreamed possible and made me a great-grandmother!

Andrew Bash's willingness to share his experiences during many years of bullying have served as an education to untold numbers of individuals and as an inspiration to all who work in the field of bullying prevention.

Could not ask for a better mentor than author and publisher Joel Goldman. His willingness to share his enormous knowledge and talent in both areas knows no bounds, and his "always being there" was most helpful as I traveled through uncharted waters.

To the members of Beth Shalom Sisterhood Banishing Bullying Behavior Project, you are truly inspiring in your response to the "call to action." These women and men share their talent with children K-12 as well as adults. They make presentations as well as conduct interactive sessions for classes of twenty and thirty and school assemblies with hundreds of students. You can read about this group in more detail in the Appendix.

To all the men and women who sought me out to share their stories in order to spare others the pain they endured, thank you.

At age 102 Regina Pachter is an inspiration to all who know her. She still plays the piano an hour a day and was recently featured on NPR.

I am most grateful for her hospitality in her lovely retirement community and the many hours she spent with me sharing her childhood bullying experience.

I had heard about Christina Sullivan's expertise, talent, and skill when it comes to design and layout. I am so appreciative that I and the readers of this book are now the beneficiaries of those professional attributes.

My sincere gratitude to Monica Watrous for sharing her expert proofreading skills in the final stages of this manuscript. Her thoughtful expertise helped produce a book with a professional finish.

I am most grateful to Moira Mulhern, Ph.D., co-founder and executive director of Turning Point: The Center for Hope and Healing. Thank you to Moira, who took time from her very busy schedule to share important insights and knowledge about bullying in the field of medicine.

To Roshann Parris and her "Best Places to Work" staff, go my admiration and appreciation for their important contribution to the message of this book.

Once again, to my quintessential husband, Neil, go my thanks for love and friendship shared and our shared vision that "the best is yet to come."

Made in the USA
Columbia, SC
20 May 2021